What Can I Do for God?

ISBN:978-1-950252-11-4

What Can I Do for God?

Learning to Store

Our Treasures in Heaven

By Summer McClellan

To
my mom,
Peggy Hickson

Contents

Forward

After reading my friend Summer's book, *The Impossible Marriage,* I was amazed at her ability to condense so many valuable keys and principles, that took me to a depth in God I did not know existed. When she wrote another book my thought was, "What more is there to say, after all, her story had been told?"

From the very first page of, *What Can I Do for God?* I was surprised that once again I hung on every word. But something was different...knowing of her tumultuous years of struggles and trials, I thought it may be that this book was necessary to share the proverbial calm after the storm. Or perhaps this book would be a way to tie up loose ends and finish her story, but it is so much more than that.

What I found in, *What Can I do for God?* is that Summer's story has only begun! I learned that her time in training, "Boot Camp" so to speak, each of her experiences, hardships and victories are collected and have stored up in this book, a treasure chest, a wealth of knowledge. Now the treasure chest is open, and has become available to us, the readers.

This book has cleared a way for me and showed me the light shining through at the end of my personal time of wilderness. It has sparked a new hope in me, and I have learned through Summer there is great purpose for each phase of my life, whether I be in a valley or on a mountain top. I have heard the wilderness experience described as a time to bring us from, "What can God do for me?" to a time of "What can I do for God?"

I have read this book slowly and carefully, knowing in it is the very heart and thoughts of God. Summer has shared with a clarity that could only come from someone close to God's heart. Someone who not only experienced going through, but also comes out.

Who is this coming up from the Wilderness, leaning upon her Beloved? Song of Solomon 8:5

Patty Szabo

Preface

When I was young and a new Christian, I was wondering about my life ahead of me. I was very disconnected from my feelings and wasn't sure what I wanted out of life. I would live my life a lot through the books I would read. I would read many exciting books about Christian Bible smugglers or missionaries and many other outstanding Christians. As I would read their books, I would be them. I would feel like them and I read constantly so, I frequently felt like some Christian hero. I tried to read every famous Christian's biography out there. I think I almost thought I was going to have a life like that; after all I was a Christian too.

God must have some magnificent plan for me, I thought, kind of like a fairy tale. {No, I was not in reality.} Then there was the real me, shy and out of reality. I was barely even functional. I was not a Christian hero; I had never even led anyone to the Lord. There was this huge gap; super spiritual imaginary me and then across this great divide the real me, sort of, shy, full of fear and always hiding, literally.

I had these secret dreams that God was going to use me in some miraculous way. I wasn't too worried that I had no education, no motivation, no skills or that I felt I was in way over my head in every area of my life. I thought God was just somehow going to do everything. I kept waiting for this miracle to happen. I would suddenly, somehow, be a superhero Christian, a magnificent soul winner. The problem was when I tried to tell people about the Lord, I became tongue-tied. I think

I did more harm than good, but I wanted to be used by God so badly!

My only picture of being used by God was to be a Billy Graham type of figure, a super soul winner, an outgoing wonder Christian. The problem was I wasn't Billy Graham. I didn't fit into what I thought being used by God was. When is this huge transformation going to take place?   I kept waiting.

When I was twenty years old, a new mother and still very shy, I decided the time had come, I had to start. There was a real sinner that lived across the street in our mobile home park named Sam. He lived in the trailer next to my mother's. He had recently retired and spent his time drinking. He was a sinner and proud of it. Every time I would pray, I thought of him. I decided to go and tell him about Jesus.

I was terrified but I was determined to be used by God. I crossed the street, but I only got as far as my mother's house. I paced around her living room for a couple of hours trying to get the courage to go next door and talk to Sam about the Lord. Finally, I decided I had to go, I wanted God to use me! I was like I turtle trying to find the courage to stick her head out of her shell.

Trembling I went next door, knocked, and asked for Sam. I opened my mouth and started to tell him," When I pray, I see your ff...."

I was going to say more but he cut me off with a stream of cuss words. Then he turned and went into his trailer and slammed the door, leaving me standing there. I felt so foolish. Everyone inside his house heard us and I could hear them roaring with laughter through the open window.

I tried to hold back the tears until I could get out of there, but I couldn't. I was too devastated. I didn't have the strength or courage to walk across the street to my house; I wanted to hide, so I stumbled back to my mother's. I could still hear the laughter from next door, from my mother's living room. I stayed there until my husband came and walked me home. I didn't come out of my house for days.

I failed.

Could I ever be used by God?
Am I just too broken, to useless
What does God want from us?
Is it possible to please Him?
How can I live for Him?

I had a lot to learn. I am writing this book for you.

Do you have a picture of what being a Christian should be and you just don't fit it?

Do you want to live for God? Do you want to store up your treasures in Heaven?

I have learned since then, a little more about being used by God, and what is important to Him. I have some good news for you. You can be used by God. Please read on....

Chapter One

Who Am I?

But Moses said, "Who am, I that I should go to Pharaoh, and that I should bring the children of Israel out of Egypt?" Exodus 3:11

Who am I? I can relate to that statement. I have always felt like a nobody. I can relate to Moses and how he felt. I grew up feeling like a nobody. How could God use me? I was fourteen when I got saved. I felt un-usable. I knew I wasn't pretty; I had frizzy hair, thick glasses and thick eyebrows. I wasn't popular. I was shy. Boys didn't like me. I had written myself off. God doesn't look at me the same way I look at myself.

Moses Asks God "Who Am I?

Moses had written himself also. He no longer fit in with the Egyptians and he didn't fit in with the Hebrews either. He was comfortable out in the desert. He had no idea that he was the deliverer the Hebrew slaves were waiting for. Obviously, God knew Moses was capable of leading the children of Israel out of Egypt, but Moses didn't feel capable.

When God, from the burning bush, commanded Moses to go to bring His people out of Egypt, he and God had a little argument; Moses was so convinced he couldn't do what God was asking. He told God he couldn't do it because he was slow of speech. This made God a little angry and He asked Moses, "Who has made man's mouth? Or who makes the mute, the deaf, the seeing or the blind? Have not I, the Lord? Now therefore go, I will be with your mouth and teach you what you shall say."

I like God's answer to Moses. We may write ourselves off. We know others think we are worthless too. Doesn't God realize we are useless? He doesn't seem to. We see others as worthless also. It could be their looks, or they aren't very smart, or they are poor or clumsy. We are trained to think like the world. God had to retrain me.

What God Looks for in a Person

I remember one time when I was about seventeen years old, I was driving home from school, and I even remember what road I was on. God started speaking to me. He asked me, "Do you know what I look for in a person?" He continued, "It is not what they look like that matters to Me and it is not their intellect. I don't care how smart someone is. It is not their personality or how much money someone has. It is their heart, their spirit that matters to Me."

God was showing me what matters. I was young and growing up in a society that teaches us the opposite of God's values, beauty, talent, fame, brains, money, that's what makes us worthwhile in our world. God was teaching me the truth; He was teaching me how He sees things.

Then God showed me a little boy who went to our church. He was mentally retarded. Even though this little boy was retarded, he seemed especially happy and was very loving. God showed me he had developed his spirit. His little mind wasn't able to develop much but his spirit had developed and matured, and he was loving and joyful. This little boy had an especially beautiful spirit to God. God told me this is often the case when someone is retarded; they develop their spirit instead of their mind. We think it is so tragic that someone is mentally retarded, because they may not be able to ever be self – sufficient financially in this life. As God was speaking to me, He was showing me things that were opposite to my way of thinking. God then spoke to me about abortion; He said, "It is never okay to abort a child, because it is the spirit of a man that is important to Me."

Our worldly thinking is so opposite to God's that many people think a retarded child should be killed in the womb. Their Creator disagrees. I needed retraining and God was retraining me. God is always right and if our thinking doesn't line up with His, then we are the one who is wrong, not God! It always surprises me when I am talking to people, and they tell me something contrary to the word of God. One lady said to me, "Don't worry about Hell, there is no Hell, God would never do a thing like that."

The Bible tells us of Hell, it warns us. You can't make up your own truth. Our world has an alternate truth, we value things that are unimportant to God, and we see things as worthless that God deems important. God is always right and the sooner we realize that the better. It is more important for you to please God than anyone else. He is the most important relationship you have; He is your Creator! We need to learn how to value the things He values and see things from His perspective.

Have You Rejected Yourself?

Have you rejected yourself like I did as a child? God is not interested in you because of how you look. You aren't too ugly or too fat and you are not too stupid or too poor. {God does not need your money}. Your disabilities will not keep Him away and you're not too old even if you are past ninety. God is looking at your heart, your spirit, the essence of who you are. God loves you, He created you and He has a plan for your life. He knows what you are capable of, He knows what you can become, in Him, and you are not disqualified.

Moses was wrong about himself. Look how

magnificently he was used by God. I have a cassette tape I have worn out about a pastor from India who had a vision of Heaven and Hell. My favorite part is his visit to Heaven. I love hearing about people who have seen Heaven, the golden streets, and the beautiful sights. This man had such an experience and while he was there, he met some of the saints. One was Moses; he had an interesting conversation with Moses. Moses told him "The first forty years of my life I thought I was something, the next forty years of my life I found out I was nothing. The last forty years of my life I found out that God could take nothing and use it for something."

Are you telling God, "Who am I?" Are you rejecting yourself because you don't see any worth in yourself or because someone else has rejected you or maybe because of past mistakes? When I hit mid-forties, I rejected myself again. It seemed like my life was over, I felt too old, too fat and too poor. God told me "You have rejected yourself, but I haven't rejected you."

I asked God to show me how He saw me. He told me to look on the cover of my Bible. I have a Precious Moments Bible. The artwork on the cover is a sweet little girl on her knees in prayer, she has a sweet smile, and she is surrounded by flowers. Just looking at her gives me a feeling of sweetness. God told me that is how I look to Him. He doesn't see overweight and wrinkles and hair that is starting to turn grey, He sees the essence of our being. He sees sweetness when He looks at me.

Are you like Moses and I, are you asking, "Who am I?" You can be loved and used by God; you are beautiful and special to Him. He has created you for a special purpose and you can do what He calls you to do.

"But the Lord said to Samuel, "Do not look at his appearance or at the height of his stature, because I have refused him. For the Lord does not see as man sees; for man looks at the outward appearance, but the Lord looks at the heart." Samuel 16:7

Chapter Two

Love the Lord Your God

You shall love the Lord your God with all your heart, with all your soul and with all your mind. This is the first and greatest commandment. And the second is like it; you shall love your neighbor as yourself. Matthew 22:37-39

The first and greatest commandment is to love the Lord your God. Knowing the most important commandment is a milestone in our quest to live for God. First things come first. I find it easy to love someone awesome and powerful and wonderful. All it takes to love God is to get a glimpse of Him. When we see Him as He is, it fills us with awe, and we can't help but obey this commandment.

I remember when I was a stupid teenager. I don't know how anyone could stand me, including God. I thought it was important to have a boyfriend, I thought it would give me some self-worth. This particular night I was sitting on my bed crying. I was crying because a boy I knew was moving away. I didn't really like him very well, but he was sort of a boyfriend. I just liked it that he liked me; I wanted to be liked.

Only someone who knows and understands the heart of a confused fifteen-year-old, that felt worthless, could possibly understand why I was miserable.

God knows about fifteen-year-old girls, he understands their ridiculous feelings and He cares. There I was sitting on my bed sobbing away and praying. When God for a split second pulled back a curtain, a curtain between our world and His, and He showed me His heart.

I saw Him, He was crying too. He was crying with me. He was so in tune with my feelings, and He was so moved by my feelings that His pain was greater than my pain.

I gasped in amazement.

His heart was broken for me. He understood me. I immediately stopped crying and wanted to comfort Him. "I am okay" I told Him, feeling so much better and amazed at His love for me. My feelings as immature as they were, were completely precious to God. I will never forget that split second for as long as I live. I realized how loving our Father is, it is easy to love Him.

Worship Touches God's Heart

We can show God, we love Him in many ways, such as worship. Worship is a fulfillment of the greatest commandment. Worship touches the heart of God. Worship is more than just singing to God with adoration in your heart. Although the worship that comes from your heart to God's heart, is invisible and intangible to you in our realm, in the realm of the spirit, it is a substance that reaches and touches God in a special way. It is desirable to Him and pleases Him. God can seem so far away, but our worship travels to Him and literally touches Him. It carries with it a piece of us that reaches out and ministers our love to Him. Worship is spiritual, it must come from our spirit, and when it does it reaches out to His Spirit.

I want to quote a portion of a book called, *The Call,* by Rick Joyner, one of my favorite authors and one of my favorite books. This passage gives us a little glimpse of our worship from a higher view. From Jesus eyes, as He sees it touch the Father. This passage is a conversation, between the author and Jesus, about worship.

"When even the most humble church sings to My

Father with true love in their hearts, He silences all of heaven to listen to them. He knows that one cannot help but worship when they are beholding His glory here, but when those who are living in such darkness and difficulty sing with true hearts to Him, it touches Him more than all the myriads of heaven can. "Many times, the broken notes from earth caused all of heaven to weep with joy as they beheld My Father being touched. A few holy ones struggling to express their adoration for Him has many times caused Him to weep. Every time I see my brethren touch Him with true worship, it makes the pain and grief I knew on the cross seem like a small price to pay. Nothing brings Me more joy than when you worship My Father. I went to the cross so that you could worship Him through Me. It is in this worship that you the Father and I are all one."

Does that excite you as much as it excites me? How incredible that we can bring such joy to the heart of the Father. How exciting we can bring such fulfillment to Jesus, when He sees our worship touching the heart of the Father. Worshipping God is a way to love Him with all our hearts. Could our first and most important thing to learn about our service to God, be to love and minister to God? YES! Do you find it exciting that you can touch your Creator's heart, with your love and worship? I do!

Loving God Through Others

Another way we can show love to God is to show love to those that He loves. God loves His children. {God loves everybody.} I relate to God on this point. If someone is mean to one of my kids, I DON'T LIKE THEM!!!!! Just call me mother bear. Do not mess with my kids! But if one of my kids needs help and someone helps them out, they are helping me. It is just like doing it to me and you are forever on my good list. I won't forget it, ever. It is the same way with God. When one of His kids are hurting and you help them out, Papa Bear is pleased. You have done it to Him. In fact, even a cup of cold water will

16

not go unrewarded. Do you want to reach out and love God? Then love one of His kids.

One night, I wanted so badly to show love to God. I thought of a way. My little girl, Joy was going to sleep next to me. She always liked it when I would stroke her hair at night. It would help her fall asleep, but my hands would get tired. This night I wanted to show the Lord love so, I told Him, "I am loving You through Joy."

As I stroked Joy's hair, I pictured Jesus. I stroked her hair {His}, until I thought my arm would fall off. As I did this, I pictured Jesus and told Him I loved Him. Joy of course loved it and drifted off to sleep.

Joy wasn't the only one who loved it because I literally felt the Lord's arms come and wrap themselves around me. It was such a wonderful feeling; I felt warm arms holding me. I never wanted it to end. It was wonderful,

I have never had that happen again, but it was amazing, the Lord loved me right back. Of course, there are endless ways to show God love through others. Simply find someone in need and help them, out of love for their Father. Tell God, "I am loving You, through them."

Abraham a Good Example

Abraham was one of the greatest examples in the Bible of a man showing his love for God. He showed love for God by amazing obedience and putting God above everything and everybody else. Remember in the Bible when God asked Abraham to sacrifice Isaac, his precious son. Abraham didn't question God, he just obeyed. I think it would have been much easier for Abraham to lay down his own life than the life of his son. God definitely was first in Abraham's life. Of course, God sent an angel to stop Abraham before he harmed his son. Abraham pleased God, he touched God's heart with his willingness to put Him above all else. You can do this too, put Him first in your life. Abraham fulfilled the first and greatest commandment, loving God.

Summer's Night of Worship

One night I had off from work, so, I decided I was going to stay up all night and worship God. I had a seven-disc, C.D. player and I loaded the whole thing with worship music. Everyone in the family was snug in their beds except my son James; he had gone on a trip to Missouri. He went to visit a Bible college he was thinking about attending. I was alone in the living room and ready to worship God all night long.

My heart was right, but before too long I fell asleep. I woke up about two a.m. and the worship music was still going. I felt an awesome, overwhelming presence of God in the room.

I am one that can never get enough of God, but this was enough. In fact, it was too much! God's presence was so strong I literally felt like I was going to die! My body was shaking and convulsing. I could not speak but in my mind, I said, "God I love Your presence, but it is going to kill me."

I wondered if this is where the phrase "holy roller" came from, maybe someone had gone through what I was going through. My body was involuntarily jerking and shaking all over. I was having such a sense of God's holiness and such a sense of my own humanness. I realized, next to God, I was not even close to being holy.

I thought of a conversation I had just had with a girl at work, she was telling me she didn't need to be saved because she was a good person. I could sense there, in God's extreme and powerful holiness, that all my righteousness was filthy rags, it became apparent to me that God's presence was terrifyingly holy, and we don't even have a chance without the blood of Jesus.

This experience lasted for some time but waned some {thank the Lord}. About five o 'clock in the morning my son, James came in, he had just driven back from Missouri, and saw me lying there on the floor. I tried to speak to him, but I could only stutter out one word "Gggodd" I managed to sputter.

James started sobbing and knelt down on the floor. "I

feel Him too," he cried out.

I am not sure why God blessed me so with His presence that night, but I wonder if it was because of my pitiful attempt to stay up and worship Him all night.

What can I do for God? I can keep the first and greatest commandment. I can love Him with all of my heart, soul and mind, I can worship Him, and I can put Him first like Abraham did. I can also bless Him by blessing His kids. I can do something amazing for God I can touch His heart!

Chapter Three

Winning the War, Conquering Self

"Woe to you scribes and Pharisees, hypocrites! For you cleanse the outsides of the cup and dish, but inside they are full of extortion and self- indulgence. Blind Pharisee first clean the inside of the cup and dish, that the outside of them may be clean also." Matthew 23:25-26

And why do you look at the speck in your brother's eye, but do not consider the plank in your own eye? Or how can you say to your brother, 'Let me remove the speck out of your eye; and look a plank is in your own eye? Hypocrite! First remove the plank from your own eye and then you will see clearly to remove the speck out of your brother's eye." Matthew 7:3-5

Before we can change the world for God there is a huge war to be won; the war within us. How can this be so important? We can't help anyone else if we are living in sin. We need to face ourselves head on and tackle the issues within ourselves. I am talking about sin. I am talking about lust, pornography and sex sin, either in the thought life or acted upon. I am talking about anger, greed, selfishness and unforgiveness. I am talking about alcohol, marijuana, drugs, prescription drug abuse and smoking. I am talking about self-centeredness, self- righteousness, pride, prejudice, sin, sin, sin. We need to deal with our sin! It is a holy war that you can win. Win it for God. Win it for yourself. Win it for your children!

Samson the Superhero

Let us look at Samson, in the Bible. God gave Samson superhuman strength so he could free the Israelites from the Philistines. He had superhuman strength, a real-life superhero. But he was taken out and lost his power, but it was not by kryptonite, and he was not brought down by the Philistines. Samson was brought down by his own lusts, Samson had a woman problem.

He picked up with a harlot named Delilah. After she nagged him constantly, he broke down and told her that the secret to his strength was that his hair had never been cut. Delilah having been paid by the Philistines, shaved Samson's head while he slept. He woke up and his superpowers were gone. His enemies, the Philistines gouged out his eyes and put him in chains. Samson became a slave in prison.

Sin will blind you. Sin will wrap its chains around you and imprison you. Sin can seem like a small thing, no big deal, you think you can control it, but it is not a small thing and like cancer it needs to be cut off completely.

Dealing with Sin

We have seen sin in the body of Christ; we have seen huge ministries fall as their leaders fall into sin. We wonder how ministers can get up and preach the gospel when secretly they commit adultery or other sins. Some have lost ministries;

others have died, and many innocent people are hurt in the process.

We have to deal with ourselves. We have to deal with our sins. We have to put up a fight and not give up. There are so many more consequences to sin than we realize. It hurts us and it hurts others. We are our children's spiritual protection. We are their covering. What about them? Do we want to open them up to be attacked in these same areas? This is what generational curses are, sins passed down from generation to generation.

My husband Jim's whole family line were alcoholics. I interviewed my father in law before he died; he died of cirrhosis of the liver, from alcohol. I asked my father in law how his mother died. He told me she died of cirrhosis of the liver, also his father died of cirrhosis of the liver, and every family member he could remember died of cirrhosis of the liver from alcohol. My husband's whole family line are alcoholics.

When the evil spirit of alcoholism came to my husband it got a fight, a knock down dragged out fight. My husband has fought alcoholism. He has tried over and over to quit on his own. He has gotten prayer hundreds of times; he has checked himself into treatment ten times; he has gone on Antabuse several times. It has taken him many years to beat it. He would fail but he would just keep trying.

I remember one time Jim and I ran into an old friend named Bill from church that we hadn't seen in about eighteen years. This friend, Bill had known us when our son had been a toddler. Jim was so proud at the time because our son was in Bible School, he told Bill about it. Bill knowing of Jim's struggles with alcohol looked surprised and then he looked at me and said to Jim, "I know Summer had something to do about that."

I thought about it for a while." Yah, I must have had a lot to do with that." I told myself, thinking of all the times I spent teaching my son the Bible when he was little. I was proud also, that he was in Bible School. The Lord interrupted my thoughts.

"It wasn't you, Summer," He told me, "It was Jim. The

devil can't get past him. Jim won't stop fighting. Jim hasn't won yet, he keeps falling, but he won't stop fighting. Satan can't destroy your children's lives like he has Jim's family line, because he can't get past Jim."

Even though sometimes, it looked like Jim's battle with alcohol was hopeless, it wasn't, because he was still fighting. If you haven't stopped fighting you haven't lost! In fact, if you never stop fighting you win!

Fight for yourself and fight for children after you, and their children. You pass on blessings, instead of curses. And do not start curses in your family line, fight sin!

I heard a minister preach on sin many years ago. He said he has seen children get sick and some die when their fathers were committing adultery. I thought that was strange, but I have seen it happen too. Even in the Bible, King David and Bathsheba's child died. How could God allow something like that?

He does not.

We allow it when we sin. The spiritual covering that God has placed over the children, has vacated his position. We cannot blame God for the results of our sin. The father is the spiritual covering. {I believe the mother can take up this position if the father has laid it down.} Do not open your family to an attack from the enemy, fight sin!

Bob Jones' Vision

Bob Jones, a wonderful prophet and man of God, in his taped vision about Heaven and Hell, speaks of seeing people wrapped in the things that bound them in life. Bob had an aneurism that broke in his abdomen and he experienced death. He saw people entering eternity that died at the same time he did.

He saw people going down on what looked like an escalator descending into darkness. These people were wrapped in what they had served on earth. He saw some wrapped in dollar bills, he saw some encased in whiskey bottles. He even saw some of them wrapped up in their lawns that were more important to them than going to church on Sunday. It made me think, we have to deal with these things, NOW, before they destroy our souls. Our biggest battle is the one within ourselves.

One Man's Battle with Himself

Some people don't have serious sin to battle, they battle complacency. They still need to conquer self. David Wilkerson writes in his Christian classic, *The Cross and the Switchblade,* how his life changed completely when he sold his television set.

David Wilkerson was a successful preacher in a small farming community. After a long day he would watch television for a few hours to help him unwind. The idea struck him "What if I sold my television and used that time in prayer every night." He wasn't sure he really wanted to do that, so he put God to the test. He decided to put an ad in the evening paper and give God exactly thirty minutes from the time the paper arrived, to sell the television. If the television didn't sell in thirty minutes, he would keep it. He told his wife Gwen about it.

"You don't want to sell that television very badly," was her reply.

So, the next day at four thirty the paper arrived. There sat David on the living room couch with his alarm clock, and his wife, Gwen, and his children looking on. After twenty-nine minutes had passed, David thought he was going to get to keep his television set. At four fifty-nine, only one minute to go, his telephone rang.

The man on the other end of the line asked, "Do you still have a television for sale?"

"Yes," David answered.

"How much is it?" he asked.

David hadn't even thought of a price. "One hundred dollars," he replied making one last feeble attempt to keep his television.

"I will take it," the man replied and then added, "I will be right over."

It was during his new two-hour prayer time, in the evenings which David used to spend watching television that his life was totally thrown off guard. As he was in his office praying, a picture from the Life magazine began to haunt him. It was a picture of seven young men on trial for murder, they were all teen-agers. The young men were part of a street gang called the Dragons. After the boys brutally stabbed another fifteen-year-old boy, they wiped his blood through their hair and bragged, "We messed him up good." The gangs of young hoodlums were taking over New York.

"Go there," the Lord whispered to his heart.

David had never even been to New York. David went to New York and led many young gang members to the Lord. Some even became ministers. That was the beginning of a Teen Challenge, a wonderful ministry that is still going more than fifty years later. It has helped countless of hopeless addicts and gang members get off drugs and live a life for the Lord. It started when one man, sold his television set, and pressed into God. He conquered himself.

It is much easier to relax in front of a television every night, than to spend several hours in prayer, but because of it, thousands of lives have been changed.

It is a holy war. Conquer self. God can't do this for you, He will help you, but this is a war you have to fight. If you don't give up, you will win. It pleases God when we fight sin in our lives, and we conquer ourselves.

We can do this!

Chapter Four
Doing the Things That Last

For no other foundation can anyone lay than that which is laid, which is Jesus Christ. Now if any one builds on this foundation with gold, silver, precious stones, wood, hay or straw, each one's work will become manifest; for the Day will declare it, because it will be revealed by fire; and the fire will test each one's work, of what sort it is. If any one's work which he has built on it endures, he will receive a reward. If any one's work is burned, he will suffer loss; but he himself will be saved yet so as through fire. 1 Corinthians 3:11-15

Our salvation has been paid for us by the blood sacrifice of Jesus. We are saved by faith in what He has done. But our lives on earth must not be wasted. Paul talks about those who build on the foundation {our salvation, our Savior Jesus Christ} those who build with gold, silver and precious stones have lived a life that counts for God. Those who have built with wood, hay and straw have wasted their lives on earth; they have done things with no lasting value. They are still saved but as those who are escaping through fire. We need to be doing the works, in our lives, that please the Lord, the things that last for eternity.

Building for Eternity

In the wonderful book, *Paradise the Holy City and the Glory of the Throne, a* man named Seneca Sodi was told about just such a thing. This book was written over a hundred years ago and is about Seneca Sodi, who was taken to Heaven in a chariot by angels. {My kind of book, I love reading about Heaven.} After Seneca arrives in Heaven, he sees other chariots arriving from earth bringing new arrivals to Heaven. Many arrive dressed in beautiful robes and jump out of the chariots praising God.

Then he sees another chariot arrive, it is carrying a woman from earth, she is clothed only in a thin robe. She gets out of her chariot and falls on the ground, she cries out in shock for she is unprepared to be there, in Heaven. The angels assure her she is in Heaven and there has been no mistake, but she is told that she is saved as through fire. She is told that during her life she did not build with gold, silver or precious stones but with wood, hay and straw. Seneca asks about her; I will quote the book.

I now said to the elder by my side, "Will you explain to me her great mistake?"

"Surely," he replied. "She represents a very large class in the world who have not made good use of earthly opportunities, she was never deeply interested in her salvation until near the time of her death. Do you see how slim and lean she looks, and how little clothing she has, only a gown! Her repentance has been genuine, and her faith accepted the promises of eternal life in her Lord, and her forgiveness has been complete. She has added but little grace and almost no growth to her soul. She feels now, as all such souls do and must feel, her great loss. She has no treasure laid up in Heaven. Paradise itself seems too good for her; but God in His great mercy will bring her on. These trees are for her. Their leaves are full of healing virtue. No one who has not received the gift of eternal life and been born again will ever be carried by the angels to this glory.

Many, alas perish from the earth in sight of the Redeemer's outstretched arms of love and mercy, because they will not accept His gracious help; they love the pleasures of sin more than God or these everlasting joys and pleasures at his right hand here forevermore."

"Oh, blessed Christ," I cried "Filled with everlasting love and mercy for thy people, that even in the last moments of life, like the dying thief, may be snatched from the jaws of death. But, oh, her great loss, how sad!"

Jesus told his disciples, *"You did not choose Me, but I chose you and appointed you that you should go and bear fruit and that your fruit should remain". Matthew 15:16*

Jesus wants us to bear fruit that remains. So how can we do the things that last? What is so important to God? How can we know how to please Him? God has been putting this lesson together in me, over the years little by little piece by piece and I still have only a glimpse, but I want to know how to do the things that please God, how to do the things that remain, how to store up treasures in Heaven.

God Judges Differently than We Do

I have learned a lot being married to my husband. I touched on this in my first book, *The Impossible Marriage.* God told me he had a much higher place in Heaven than I did. This blew my mind because my husband, Jim, in my mind, was such a sinner. I saw his police record once in the district attorney's office, a lawyer who was helping Jim, asked me to go there and request some information. I couldn't believe Jim's record, it started as an early teenager, it was very long, and they had him classified as the highest risk and dangerous.

At the time the Lord told me that Jim had a high place in Heaven, Jim was a drinking alcoholic and had recently committed another crime and was facing another prison sentence! How could he be more pleasing to God than me? I read my Bible and listened to Christian tapes all day long. I never missed church, I tithed, I thought I was a real saint and

Jim was a real sinner!

I had to learn to see as God sees and to understand what it is that is important to Him. The Lord showed me that my husband was extremely humble before Him and also whenever the Lord would tell my husband to do something, my husband would do it. I on the other hand was proud and rarely obedient.

He also showed me that Jim had huge problems, demonic spirits, that the Lord called giants, to overcome and Jim was using everything inside himself, all his effort, and although Jim seemed to be losing the battle, he wasn't, because he never quit and the results just took years to see.

When it comes to God, Jim had always used all his effort. Even as a child, my husband, Jim would go to church alone, he walked by himself across town, in Detroit, to his favorite church. He won an award for perfect attendance.

This really blows my mind to think about. Here Jim, was abused as a child; he had started life with everything against him, and yet, this troubled little boy, from a non-church going family, got himself up and ready, every Sunday morning, and walked several miles through down town Detroit, by himself, to get to church every Sunday. And on top of everything else, he had perfect attendance.

Most kids from church-going families have to be poked and prodded to get ready on time and then their parents bring them and go with them. Jim was different.

God sees hearts. He sees the amount of effort we put in serving Him. A small thing that takes all our effort is bigger than a big thing that took little effort. Remember the widow's mite. Jesus and His disciples were watching different people putting money in the temple treasury. When a widow came and put in half of a penny Jesus told his disciples she put in more than all the others, she had given all she had! {Mark 12:41-44}

God also loves humility and obedience, living this way produces fruit that will last. We can't judge others because we can't see their hearts. God sees hearts and a humble heart pleases Him.

Giving is very important, when doing things that last;

Paul was more concerned about the Philippians when they sent him a gift, than he was about himself. He wanted to see them doing the things that last.

Giving Cheerfully

For even in Thessalonica, you sent me aid once and again for my necessities. Not that I seek the gift, but I seek the fruit that abounds to your account. Philippians 4:15-16

Paul is talking about their heavenly account, he wants them laying up treasure in Heaven. Our attitude in giving is very important, giving cheerfully.

So, let each one gives as he purposes in his heart, not grudgingly or of necessity; for God loves a cheerful giver. 2 Corinthians 9:7

I learned this lesson one time when my mother's car broke down. For several years I had been driving an ancient sixteen-year-old Chevy Caprice station wagon, Babe the Big Blue Ox, we called it.

One day my son brought a man home with a car for sale, he only wanted one thousand dollars for it. I fell in love with it immediately. It was a Mercury Sable station wagon, it was from the same decade, and it had windows that went up and down, a quality my old car did not have. I wanted the new car, it seemed like a Rolls Royce to me. The man gave me a little time to come up with the money, so I bought it. All of a sudden, I felt like Cinderella with a golden chariot, {silver}.

As soon as I got my new car, my mother's car broke down and she needed to borrow a car. I wouldn't have minded a bit loaning her my old car, but I wanted to drive my new car. I did it to myself, I felt guilty loaning her the old car, so I loaned her the new one. I made no one happy, I was miserable I wanted to drive my new car, my mom couldn't figure out how anything on the dash worked and wished I would have loaned her my old car because she had driven it before and was used to it.

Then the Lord spoke to me, He said "Summer, I would

have preferred you let your mother drive the older car because you could have given it joyfully." I was surprised because I thought I did the better thing, the more generous thing. I learned something; God wants a cheerful giver, not a grumpy giver. I would have been better off letting her use the older car because I could have been a cheerful giver.

Doing Things that Remain

Let's talk more about doing things that last. One of my favorite books is called *Angels on Assignment* and is written by Roland Buck a pastor. The book tells of his visits from angels and what he learns.

In Pastor Roland Buck's book *Angels on Assignment* one of the angels gave him a message about the Believers Judgment. "The Believers Judgment is a good day," the angel told him, "It is a day when God says thanks."

The angel talked to Pastor Buck about doing things that remain. He told him there are many things that have value on earth, but they have no eternal value. He spoke of giving campaigns. He said if you give for credit, you get your reward here, but not in Heaven. God wants giving from the heart. He spoke of books that are written and sermons that are preached which may have value, but they don't speak to the needs of people. They have a reason here, but they don't last.

God's heart is people; He is where people have needs. God is where people are hurting, when we, in love, meet the needs of people we are doing things that remain. I will quote some of the book.

The angel said it was more important to be like Jesus, in the area of meeting a person's need, than to be witnessing to people about salvation. That really surprised me. We have become so conditioned to the idea that we aren't doing anything for God unless we are able to get out and witness and skillfully use the Word. But this angel said, "When you are helping people, you become a living word to them which says, 'I care, and God cares for you!' "That

doesn't mean we exalt ourselves as Jesus; it simply means Jesus is living His life through us. We become a word that is alive to them, not a dead, printed word, but a living word. This is something we can do, and it is more important than witnessing, quoting scripture or teaching. Instead of witnessing we BECOME a witness of what Jesus is really like. This is something everyone can do! We don't have to have a special talent to lay up treasure in Heaven. Any Christian can make a deposit in the bank of Heaven every day, because there are people who need help every day. When we care for them, we are bringing the heart of God to them in their place of need. When we do this for God something goes into our account!

We are learning the things that are important to God, the things that remain. God is pleased when we become, Him, to hurting people when we show them through our concern and actions that He loves them.

We are learning that we want to lay up for ourselves treasures in Heaven. And that Jesus is our foundation, but we want to build on His salvation with gold, silver and precious stones.

We are learning God looks at our hearts. He can see if we are giving our all, like the widow and her mite.

We are learning our attitude is important and we need to give cheerfully. We are learning to do the things that last and what we can do for God.

Chapter Five
Doing the Things That Last - Part Two

And you He made alive, who were dead in trespasses and sin, in which you once walked according to the course of this world, according to the prince of the power of the air, the spirit who now works in the sons of disobedience, among whom we all once conducted ourselves in the lusts of our flesh, fulfilling the desires of the flesh and of the mind ,and were by nature children of wrath just as the others .Ephesians 2:1-3

We have been programmed by the spirit of this world, the devil, to want and value the things that don't last. We want money, lots of money. We want nice cars, nice houses, we want it all. Casinos are packed with cars of those who think they will win big. The big lotto jackpots sell millions and millions of tickets. Everybody wants money. We are here for a purpose, and it is not to make money and it is not to get rich. Why do we want to be so rich? Can you take it with you? No!

Now behold, one came and said to him, "Good Teacher, what good thing should I do that I might have eternal life?"

So, He said to him, "Why do you call me good? No one is good but One, that is God. But if you want to enter life, keep the commandments."

He said to Him, "Which ones?"

Jesus said, "You shall not commit murder. You shall not commit adultery, You shall not steal, you shall not bear false witness, Honor your father and your mother and You shall love your neighbor as yourself."

The young man said, "All these things I have kept from my youth. What do I still lack?"

Jesus said to him, "If you want to be perfect, go, sell what you have and give to the poor, <u>and you will have treasure in Heaven</u>; and come, follow Me."

But when the young man heard that saying he went away sorrowful for he had great possessions.

Then Jesus said to His disciples, "Assuredly I say to you that it is hard for a rich man to enter the kingdom of Heaven. Again, I say to you it is easier for a camel to go through the eye of a needle than for a rich man to enter the kingdom of God. Matthew 19:16-24

Why would we want to become rich when Jesus said it is hard for the rich man to enter the kingdom of God? I want to make into the Kingdom of God; I don't want to make it harder on myself.

I once had a pastor who always would say, "I could never become very rich because I would just keep giving my money away." I think he had the right idea. We have to stop thinking earthly and get started thinking eternally, heavenly, godly.

Jesus said, *"Do not lay up for yourselves treasures on earth where moth and rust destroy, and thieves break in and steal; but lay up for yourselves treasure in Heaven where neither moth or rust destroys and where thieves do not break in and steal. For where your treasure is there your heart will be also." Matthew 6:19-21*

Playing in the Sand

Jesus exhorted us to store up our treasures in Heaven. Storing our riches on earth is foolish, because it isn't true riches. Living just for here is a waste of time. It won't last. I love an illustration of this from the book, *The Heavens Opened,* by Anna Rountree. Anna Rountree was taken on a tour of Heaven, while she was there, she learned about herself. A small angel named Crystal Clear revealed to her, her inner motives of wanting to build on earth. I will quote the book.

"She appeared to be a child about five or six years old, but she was shining. She had no wings, and her eyes looked old beyond her years in her small stature. She wore a pale calico pinafore over a faintly colored short shift. Her hair was curly and tousled as if from play. She looked like a little girl, but every so often I could see through her arm or leg and knew her to be a spirit. She was intriguing.

Suddenly we were on a vast shoreline, but there was no sea. It looked as though the beach was still there but no ocean. In the sand were all manner of red and blue children's buckets and shovels.

"Haven't you always wanted to build a sandcastle?" she asked.

I chuckled, "Well not really, Crystal Clear."

"Yes, you have," she continued. "Think about it. You've wanted to build on earth and all of that is sand. When the tide comes in it goes away. Even the tools for building remain longer than a sandcastle, for the tools are from God. But if you use them to build on sand instead of eternity, what do you have? A waste of time," she shrugged. "You have wanted a sandcastle. It's silly really, isn't it?"

"I suppose so," I said quietly. I did not want to admit it, but she was right. I had wanted a home and financial security and to accomplish something--- for God, of course—but I had tunnel vision for the life on earth. I had Christianized the gospel of the world and bought into my own packaging. It was a bitter thing to hear that the focus of

my life had been fleshly and worthless to God, and that I had not gotten away with it.

"Do you want to play?" she continued cheerily.

I felt a little sick. I thought I would change the subject. "Why such a large sand area?" I asked.

"Many want to build on sand, so we let them. It gets it out of their systems, you know. Maybe if you build on the sand right now, you will feel, 'I've done that"

Maybe we should all go the beach and play in the sand and get it out of our systems. Even as Christians we buy into the same spirit of the world, we just put it in a Christian package. We want to be big stuff in the church world! Even the disciples missed it in this way. They wanted to be big stuff in the Christian world. The mother of James and John two of the disciples came to ask Jesus a favor. She wanted her sons to be rulers with Jesus.

Then the mother of Zebedee's sons came to Him with her sons, kneeling down and asking something from Him. And He said to her, "What do you wish?" She said to Him, "Grant that these two sons of mine may sit, one on Your right hand and the other on Your left, in Your kingdom."

But Jesus answered her and said, "You do not know what you ask. Are you able to drink from the cup I am about to drink, and be baptized with the baptism I am baptized with?

They said to Him, "We are able." So He said to them, "You will indeed drink my cup, and be baptized with the baptism that I am baptized with; but to sit on my right hand and on my left is not Mine to give, but it is for those for whom it is prepared by my Father."

And when the ten heard it they were moved with indignation against the two brothers. But Jesus called them to Himself and said, "You know that the rulers of the Gentiles rule it over them, and those who are great exercise authority over them. Yet it shall not be so among you; but whoever desires to become great among you, let him be your servant. And whoever desires to be first among you let him be your slave—just as the

Son of Man did not come to be served but to serve and to give His life as a ransom for many." Matthew 20:20-28

Jesus said to be great we have to be a servant. Even the disciples had things upside down according to eternal thinking. They wanted to be big stuff in the church world. They were, like Anna, putting worldly thinking in a Christian package. The kingdom of God doesn't operate like the world does. The thinking is totally opposite from each other. In fact, very few understood Jesus, they thought He was building an earthly kingdom, they thought He was going to be a king, and overthrow the Romans. Jesus was building a spiritual kingdom, Jesus was building for eternity, He is our example.

Things that Don't Last

Jesus wants us to be a servant! What is this all about? Let's talk some more about our worldly thinking and how we are trained to do the things that won't last. We are told from the time we are tiny we have to go to college and get an education.

WHY?

So, we can get a good job and then start saving for retirement.

WHY?

We have to have a retirement plan so we can live in ease and enjoy our retirement at the standard of living we are used to, and let's hope we don't live too long, and our money runs out.

What is it all for?

Does it prepare us for eternity?

Jesus tells in scripture about a man with a great retirement plan. *Then He spoke a parable to them, saying: "The ground of a certain rich man yielded plentifully. And he thought within himself saying 'What shall I do since I have no room to store my crops?' So, he said, 'I will do this; I will pull down my barns and build greater, and there I will store all my crops and my goods. And I will say to my soul, "Soul, you have many goods laid up for many years; take your ease eat drink and be merry." But God said to him, 'You fool! This night your soul will be required of you; then whose will those things be which you have provided?' "So is he who lays up treasure for himself and is not rich before God." Luke 12:16-21*

Am I saying, "Don't go to college, don't save for retirement?"

No, but these things are not going to last. Education is good, but it won't get you to Heaven and it isn't going to last, savings are a good thing, but they are not something that lasts; all of this is for here.

What about eternity? We need to change our thinking.

I felt so guilty because I didn't go to college. It was my parents plan; my dad had my college tuition saved. I got married instead. I carried guilt for years; I felt like a failure in that area, it was one of those things that weighed on the back of my mind. One day the Lord dealt with it.

"What have I called you to do?" the Lord asked me. I thought about it, I wanted to be a mother and I wanted to help motherless children someday too. It was in me since I was a little girl.

"You have called me to be a mother," I told the Lord.

"That is right," the Lord replied and added "Do you need to go to college for that?"

"No"

"I never intended for you to go to college," the Lord told me, taking the load of guilt off my shoulders.

God has a plan for our lives. We are here for a purpose, and it is not to build on earth, if we follow God's will for our lives, we build for eternity. I am not here to see how rich I can get or to see how much education I can get or to see how much I can save for retirement.

Food

What other things are people wasting their lives on?
Food!
Do we need to eat?

Yes.

Is food a bad thing?

NO!

Does it last; does it prepare you for eternity?

We are a people obsessed with food. I can't cook out of magazines anymore; there are ingredients I never even heard of. We have whole networks on television dedicated to food. We want every meal to be delicious. There are restaurants that cost fifty or a hundred dollars for two people to eat! Jesus tells us a story {true} about a man who fares sumptuously every day.

Here was a certain rich man who was clothed in purple and fine linen and fared sumptuously every day. But there was a certain beggar named Lazarus, full of sores, who was laid at his gate, desiring to be fed with the crumbs which fell from the rich man's table. Moreover, the dogs came and licked his sores.

So, it was the beggar died, and was carried by the angels to Abraham's bosom. The rich man also died and was buried. And being in torments in Hades, he lifted up his eyes and saw Abraham afar off and Lazarus in his bosom.

Then he cried and said, 'Father Abraham, have mercy on me, and send Lazarus that he may dip the tip of his finger in water and cool my tongue; for I am tormented in this flame.' But Abraham said, "Son, remember that in your lifetime you received your good things, and likewise Lazarus evil things; but now he is comforted, and you are tormented. And besides all this there is a great gulf fixed, so that those who want to pass from here to you cannot, nor from those from there pass to us. Luke 16:19-26

This rich man was totally surprised to wake up in Hell. He wasn't expecting to be there. He had dined sumptuously all of his life. He did not feel that Lazarus was his responsibility. He was just a poor man that sat at his gate, after all he wasn't even a relative and he was just a beggar.

How was he responsible for this beggar? Why is he in Hell? Now all he wants is a single drop of water. Was Lazarus somehow his responsibility? The rich man lived for food. Where did it get him?

Pets

I have touched on money, education, retirement, food, what else can we talk about?

Pets!

Animals have become more important than humans!

What do I mean?

There are children in this country with no parents, no homes, no food and no love. Dogs in this country have it better than many children do. They are fed better, have more toys, they have doggy doctors, doggy beauty parlors, doggy motels, dog health insurance, dog day cares and even doggy cemeteries! We are discarding murdered children in the trash and dogs are getting burials in their own cemeteries.

Dogs are not made in God's image, children are. I was waiting in my car in a parking lot at a store, while my husband was inside shopping. While I was waiting, a glitzy, well dressed, well-coiffed dog was waiting in the car next to me. A young woman came out of the store got in the car and began kissing the dog.

Why not find a child to help?!!! There are plenty around!

I have seen people spending hundreds on their pooch's health care while nieces, nephews, grandchildren go without health care or dental care and lay in bed for weeks in pain with rotten teeth.

One single mom I knew, who could barely feed her children had a well to do sister whose dog slept in a brass bed, and it ate better than her nephews too.

Am I saying we need to mistreat dogs?

No, but we need to get our priorities straight. I want you to do the things that last forever. Children are eternal beings made in God's image; pets are not! Do you feel like the rich man in Jesus' story did, that it is not your responsibility?

I recently visited a church that was participating in a program to help children. They picked a school from the poorest area of their town. They were taking volunteers from the church to volunteer for one hour every week to help a child do their homework and mentor them. The program had been going on for many years and they showed a video from some of the mentors and their students.

One of the students a young Latino man told his story of being mentored. He said, "Both my parents are alcoholics, I had no one in my home that took any interest in me. Mrs. Allen came to my school every week to help me with my schoolwork. She stayed with me all through school. She is still in my life, and we are still close. Having one person in my life that loved me, encouraged me, prayed for me and with me, has made a difference in my life. I never would have made it through school without her."

Mrs. Allen is building for eternity!

Sports and Entertainment,

I don't think I am done yet. What about sports?

We build huge stadiums, buy huge television sets and spend lots of money and time all to watch some guys and a ball. Sports aren't bad but how much time are we spending? How much money are we spending? How important do we make it? It is one of those things that don't last.

What about entertainment?

I am talking about movies and television. These people are getting huge amounts of money to pretend to do something. They aren't really doing anything. Then they have huge award ceremonies to award them for doing nothing! They all arrive in gowns that cost thousands, to get a huge amount of attention and an award.

I never watch that stuff. I think about those who deserve an award, the people that lay down their lives every day doing their best at a hard job that really helps people, like policemen and firemen and my grandson, David's teacher.

Mrs. R got my grandson for a teacher before he was three years old because he wasn't talking, and he went into the early learning program for help. Because my grandson couldn't express himself verbally, he would get frustrated and bite and scratch. For three years Mrs. R gave my grandson her all. Many times, she had bite and scratch marks on her face and neck, but her love and patience never wavered.

She doesn't get paid much and she doesn't get an Emmy award, but she is doing things that last. Yes, maybe she is just doing her job, but she is so Christ-like in the way she does her job that she has changed my grandson's life. She cried when she moved him on to kindergarten, she truly loves him. She is doing things that last. She is building for eternity.

Beauty That Lasts

Let's talk about beauty, the world values beauty. We worship beauty.

It is temporary.

The Bible says *All flesh is like grass and all its glory like the flower of grass. The grass withers and the flower falls. 1Peter1:24.*

Beauty is not something that lasts. There is a beauty that lasts though, and that is inner beauty.

The Bible speaks of an imperishable beauty. *But let your adorning be the hidden person of the heart with the imperishable beauty of a gentle and quiet spirit, which in God's sight is very precious. 1Peter3:4.*

Women and men are spending big bucks on plastic surgery, so they can be beautiful. They get face lifts and nose jobs, liposuction and breast enhancements, tummy tucks, injections in their lips, the list is almost endless. It is all for a temporary beauty that cannot last.

Women who are sixty think they have to look thirty. Young women are unhappy with their bodies too. Let me tell you something it may come as a shock. As you get older it is okay to look older. There is no shame to look sixty if you're sixty. Let's work on the beauty that lasts, the one that doesn't wilt like a flower wilts. Let us become Christ like and shine forth with an inner beauty that will never fade.

I want to tell you about a beautiful woman I met one time. She shined with beauty. Her name was Jan. I met her on my first night on a new job delivering newspapers.

I was scared, I hadn't had a job in years, and I was shy. I had to report to a garage at two a.m. in the morning to learn the job. I hadn't realized how cold it got in the night and I didn't dress warm enough. The papers were late coming off the printing press and I stood there waiting, off to myself, not talking to anyone and shivering.

Jan was sitting on her car wrapped in a bedspread. She called me over and introduced herself and then she wrapped me in her bedspread with her. Jan loved everyone. She was amazing. I would see the others we worked with come over to her car to talk when they had a problem. She listened and she cared. I rushed to her many times when I needed emotional support or a friend, we all did, the men and the women at our paper district. Ever since the night she wrapped up cold me in her blanket, I loved her.

Now I'll tell you what she looked like. Or do you even care what she looked like because she was one in a million? Jan was about late thirties, she was heavy and had long stringy black hair, she needed dental work done and had several front teeth missing. A man we worked with called her an old hag one time. He was a successful man with a good day job who ran a paper route in the night only to pay down his mortgage early. One day he lost his day job, he came in very upset. He went straight to Jan.

I heard bits and pieces of their conversation. He said, "I have been waiting all day to come and talk to you. I knew I could talk to you about it."

She was there for him too, just like she was there for the rest of us. She no longer looked like a hag to him because he saw in her someone who would listen and understand. Jan was like that. She was truly beautiful; she will be just as beautiful when she is ninety because it isn't the kind of beauty that fades.

I could go on about the things that last, and the things

that don't. I have seen grown men playing video games while their wives and children spend time alone in the same house. I have seen women on the phone constantly while their children need attention, or how about the computer?

We cannot waste our lives on earth. We need to do the things that last.

God loves people. Jesus is where hurting people are.

Do you want to build for eternity? There are plenty of opportunities! There are hurting people all around. Is there a Lazarus at your doorstep? Do you pass him by?

Jesus has bought and paid for our salvation. We are saved through faith in Him. But the material we build with must not be wood, hay and straw, they must be things that last. We need to keep looking back to our example, Jesus. His life was not about amassing a fortune, yet he had enough. His life was not about spending time in ease. He came not to be served but to serve. He came to do the works of the Father. He came to seek and save the lost. He took the narrow path all the way to the cross. He is our example. He did the things that last.

Chapter Six

We Are Made for a Purpose

For we are his workmanship, created in Christ Jesus for good works, which God prepared beforehand that we should walk in them. Ephesians 2:10

We do not need to be afraid of God's will for us. I was. I know many others have been too. We are afraid that if we put our lives totally in God's hands, He will call us to do something we will hate.

This isn't true; in fact, it is just the opposite, completely the opposite. You were made by God for a purpose. Of course, your first purpose is to be His child and to love Him. But that is not all; He has a plan for your life, a work for you to do. He made you and called you to a purpose, a purpose that fits you like a hand to a glove. You will never be happier when you are doing what you are created to do.

Noah and the Ark

I used to feel sorry for Noah. He kind of got born at a

bad time. The whole earth was wicked, and God was going to destroy the earth with a flood. Poor Noah, I thought, he had to build a huge ark, it took one hundred years, and then he had to endure the flood.

When God was teaching me that His will for each individual was pleasing and suited for each one of us, He showed me Noah.

I was so surprised.

I saw Noah in the ark as the flood started. Noah was not sitting in the corner afraid as I thought he would be. He was thrilled! I saw him pacing excitedly around the boat straining to hear the sounds of the storm. Every rock of the boat and sound of the storm excited him more. This was the epitome of his days. He was in an ark in a flood, and He LOVED It!!! I felt what he was feeling, and it was pure delight. He was being fulfilled. He was made for this. He was having his moment!

I am glad he fulfilled his destiny, and you should be too. Without his righteousness and his faithfulness to obey God, none of us would be here. We can all call Noah, grandpa.

Not only is God's will the best thing for our lives, it is the best thing for others. We all need each other; I need what you do, and you need what I do. Everything works wonderfully when everyone is doing what they were called to do. That is what Heaven will be like.

For the body is one and has many members, but all the members of that one body, being many, are one body, so also is Christ. For by one Spirit, we were all baptized into one body-whether Jews or Greeks, whether slaves or free-and have all been made to drink in one Spirit. For in fact the body is not one member but many. If the foot should say, "Because I am not a hand, I am not of the body," is it therefore not of the body? And if the ear should say, "Because I am not an eye, I am not of the body "is it therefore not of the body? If the whole body were an eye, where would be the hearing? If the whole were hearing where would be the smelling? But now God has set the members, each one of them, in the body just as He pleased. And if they were all one member, where would the body be? But now

*indeed there are many members, but one body. And the eye
cannot say to the hand, "I have no need of you"; nor again the
head to the feet, "I have no need of you." No, much rather,
those members of the body which seem to be weaker are
necessary. And those members of the body which we think to be
less honorable, on these we bestow greater honor; and our
unpresentable parts have greater modesty, but our presentable
parts have no need. But God composed the body, having given
greater honor to that part which lacks it, that there should be
no schism in the body, but that the members should have the
same care for one another. 1 Corinthians 12: 12-25*

No Unimportant Parts of the Body

This makes me think of a little old lady who used to go
to our church. We called her sister Lucy. She was as wide as she
was tall, she walked with a cane, and she had an oxygen tank
trailing behind her. If she got a hold of you, first she would grab
your hand and squeeze and then she would pull you down and
hug you, tight. Sometimes she would raise her hand to say
something during church and once she got started talking, she
would go on and on.

I used to get slightly annoyed. I am ashamed to say that
sometimes I would inwardly groan when I saw her coming.
Then she started coming to our lady's prayer meeting. It took
some getting used to. She would pray over something so long
and so hard, I would get bored. I actually thought God was
getting bored too.

He wasn't.

I had a lesson to learn. One time as we were praying, I
had a vision, I saw demons fleeing; I saw great confusion in
Satan's camp. As the demons were fleeing, they were saying,
"What is this, what is going on!" They were terrified.

Then I saw what it was, it was sister Lucy's prayers!

The Lord showed me a thing or two about sister Lucy;
she went on so long when she spoke or when she prayed
because her heart was filled with love for the people of our

church. We were her world. She prayed for us long and hard, each person, out of a heart of love, and the Lord showed me she was humble.

In fact, she was so humble she did not even pray for her own needs, she only prayed for others. The Lord was pleased with her. The Lord then showed me she was absolutely vital to our church! We NEEDED her! I needed her! My attitude changed, I wanted her praying for me! We are all part of the body. We are all necessary for the body to function.

Doing Your Job with Love

I used to think that the Pastor was the most important person in the body, and he would be the greatest in Heaven also. Then the rest of us in the church kind of lined up behind him in importance and I was somewhere at the end of that line.

This is not true.

Can the eye say to the hand, "I don't need you?" We are all important. I sure would not want to call my Pastor when my car breaks down! I don't think he would appreciate that either. I call my mechanic, Tim. I have a Christian mechanic. He is terrific. I have gone to him for many years.

My husband, Jim and I drive secondhand cars and believe me we appreciate our mechanic! I tried to tell Tim one day how much we appreciate him, and he got a puzzled look on his face and said, "I am just doing my job."

But that is not true; he does more than just do his job. He cares about all of us that bring our cars to him. He does a good job, and he does it at a good price. What a blessing to have such a godly mechanic! He is very important, and we need him.

Is he less important in the body of Christ because he is a mechanic and not a preacher? No, No, No! Are you any less important because you are a mother and a housewife or a banker or a store clerk? No, No, No!

Another thing that amazed me was finding out it is that it is not the position God puts you in that determines your place in Heaven, it is how you live, and love, and what you build your life with.

A person in the ministry does not necessarily have a higher place than my mechanic. We all have the opportunity to build our lives with gold, silver or precious stones or wood, hay and straw.

A mechanic that honors God by caring about the people whose cars he fixes, may be building with gold, where as someone, in what we tend to think of as a more spiritual position, may not be using love in his life and be building with straw. We are all important to God, from housewife to mechanic to president. You are part of the body of Christ. We can't do without you! You are important!

What can I do for God?

I can be the person He has called me to be and do the works He has for me to do, and I will be fulfilled. I can see that what He has called me to do is important! I can be close to Him for all eternity because I can serve Him with the gifts and talents, He has called me to, with LOVE.

Chapter Seven
Meeting the Needs of Your Family

Nevertheless, let each one of you in particular so love his own wife as himself, and let the wife see that she respects her husband. Ephesians 5:33

Children obey your parents in the Lord, for this is right. "Honor your father and mother," which is the first commandment with promise: "that it may be well with you and you may live long on the earth. And you fathers don't provoke your children to wrath but bring them up in the training and admonition of the Lord. Ephesians 6:1-4

The family is God's idea. The family is to be a unit dedicated to God and knit together in love. The family starts with a husband and a wife. *Husbands love your wives as Christ loves the church.*

Being a good husband is an important service to the Lord. Loving your wife is important to God. It is a commandment from God, He is expecting you to fulfill. It is between you and God, Your Creator. If you do not love your wife, don't point your finger at her and say to God, "Who could love her!" You are responsible for your actions, and you have been commanded to love your wife, that is your responsibility. Love is action. It is not living selfishly with your time or the money you earn.

Wives you are to respect your husbands. Doing the things, a wife does is your service to the Lord. Be faithful to God, and obey His commandment to you, and don't point your finger at your husband and say to God, "I would respect him if he wasn't such a jerk." No, do your part and obey God's command, being a good wife is your service to the Lord, and your home will be happy.

One Wife's Unshakable Respect

One of my all-time favorite stories out of the Guidepost magazine is about a woman who refused to disrespect her husband and she won her husband back from another woman. It is such a beautiful story of a Christian woman who respected her husband because of her faith in God and not because of his behavior.

The story is written by Calvin, a friend of the couple. In the story, Calvin is a close friend of Jerry, the husband, and Barbara, the wife, in fact he introduced them.

Calvin describes Barbara as a tall blonde with steady eyes that a man remembered, and honesty shone through like a stained-glass window.

Jerry, he describes as good looking, and girls were always falling for him.

The people in their small town, he tells us, said Barbara was too quiet and gentle for Jerry and that she was the religious type and Jerry was the wild kind.

Then Calvin describes for us Ginger, an old girlfriend of Jerry's, she is a sultry red head who would like nothing better than to break up Barbara and Jerry's marriage.

Things went smoothly until Barbara and Jerry had been married about a year. Calvin began to notice Jerry and Ginger together, here and there. In fact, the whole town began to talk. People tried to warn Barbara what was going on, but she would just smile and say, "I trust my husband."

After Calvin passed Jerry's parked car in an alley one night, and it wasn't Barbara in the car with Jerry, it was Ginger, Calvin tried to talk to Jerry. Jerry blew up in anger and told Calvin to mind his own business. Jerry told Calvin things were fine between him and Barbara and even invited Calvin and his girlfriend Nan over for dinner, to prove it.

They went to dinner, and everything seemed serene between Jerry and Barbara. But Nan, Calvin's girlfriend said to Calvin as he drove her home.

"Jerry will be a bachelor as long as he lives, and Barbara makes it easy for him. Even the notes don't seem to upset her."

"What notes," Calvin asked her.

"Some spiteful woman is sending her notes about Jerry," Nan replied.

"Does Jerry know?"

"No, Barbara tears them up. She refuses to see what everyone else sees. She just believes what she wants to believe."

Things came to a head soon after. Both couples, Nan and Calvin and Barbara and Jerry were at a Harvest Ball at their Legion Post. Just as they were going to leave, Ginger appeared at their table, partly drunk and mean as a snake. I will quote the rest of the story in Calvin's words.

"Well," Ginger said, "You're a hard one to convince."

Not one of us said a word. Barbara was perfectly calm; Jerry looked tense and grim.

"Ask him," said Ginger, still speaking to Barbara. "Ask him where he was between six and eight last Thursday night."

I stood up and put my hand on her arm. "Look Ginger," I said, "Why don't you?" She shook me off.

"All right," she said to Barbara. "So, you want proof. Well, here's the motel receipt." She flung a scrap of paper on the table. "There!" she said "Ask him to deny it! I dare you!"

Barbara looked at Ginger about ten seconds. It seemed like ten years. There was no anger in her face just serenity and confidence.

"I think you're mistaken," she said. "My husband and I love each other. We stood up in God's house and made a promise for better or worse. For richer or poorer. In sickness and in health. To love and cherish…."

She hesitated, and it was an incredible thing; you could feel the power of evil that was in Ginger shrink until it seemed insignificant and unimportant.

When Barbara spoke again it was almost as if she were speaking to a child. "The man I married," she said, "is the man I love. And the man I love is the man I married. So, I don't think he's the one you know. In fact, I'm sure he isn't. You must be talking about someone else." She turned to Nan. "Let's go, Nan."

They walked away together. Ginger stood there, her face dark with fury. "That fool!" she said.

She stamped off without another word. I looked at Jerry. If I ever saw self-loathing on a man's face it was on his. "We both know who the fool is, Cal," he said. He pounded his hand against the table. "Never," he said, "So help me never again!"

Calvin ends the story by telling us several years go by and the couple have a wonderful marriage, everything Barbara believes about Jerry, he becomes. Barbara treated her husband the way the Bible told her to, but it had nothing to do with HIS behavior.

What she did was supernatural, no one being cheated on could respond in such a godly way without help. She and God were in on that one together! She brought good to her home by her behavior. She defeated evil; she overcame!!!! Her faith dumbfounded a whole town of people who couldn't understand her response to the situation. Her service to God was how she treated her husband.

Marriage and family are holy ground. Treating your family in a godly way is part of your service to God. Husbands loving their wives and wives loving their husbands are no small thing to God. It is where we start in our quest to please God.

Parents Build for Eternity

Being a parent is a wonderful opportunity to serve the

Lord also. A child is an eternal being; and raising a child is a huge privilege.

Fathers, scripture tells you not to provoke your children but to teach them the things of God. Love your children and be patient with them. You have a huge responsibility with a huge impact. Your child is treasure you can lay up in Heaven.

Mothers, changing diapers and making meals is a holy thing. Realize in these difficult years, which do pass, that although it doesn't seem glamorous, what you are doing is important and God looks at things differently than we do. You are on holy ground. Put your all, into your little ones while you can.

I had some concept of this as a young mother, I wanted to take every advantage of the time I had with my children while they were small and teach them about the Lord. If I wavered in my commitment to them, I got a reminder of the importance and how quickly they grow and how little time we have to influence them for the good.

My reminder was from the pastor's son. When I was a teenager in church, our pastor's son was such a cute and very sweet little boy. He was incredibly precious. One year during the Christmas program this darling little tot got tired and laid down on the stage during the program and closed his eyes and went to sleep. Embarrassed his dad, the pastor, ran up to the stage and scooped him up in his arms. We all laughed and thought it was darling.

We moved away and I didn't see the little boy until years later when he was in his late teens. I had small children of my own by then and we were in town for a visit. This darling little boy was a big burly teen now and he was in full rebellion. He did NOT want to be in church and it was obvious. I could not believe this was the same kid.

Seeing the change in him drove it home to me, that I wanted to use my time, while my children were little to influence them all I could for God. And I did, I made God's love real to them so they would always want to serve Him, and they have.

The story about the pastor's son also ends well. His rebellious phase passed, and he is a fine adult. But I am thankful to have seen him, it helped me realize we need to lay a godly foundation while our kids are young and not to let that opportunity go by.

When my kids were little, my worship time was their worship time; I worshipped with them at bedtime, to kids praise music. My prayer time was their prayer time, and we read the Bible together, I read children's Bibles in those years. We had fun together.

Your family is Gods idea and being a Christian starts at home. Treat your family with care; they are not yours they are God's. A man who takes care of his family is a godly man; a woman who takes care of her family is a godly woman.

Honor Your Father and Mother

Let's move on. Honor your father and mother. This is unto God again. You may be unhappy with your parents, but this is a commandment. You do it for God. This commandment comes with a promise that it may go well with you, and you will live long on the earth. This promise even works for unbelievers. God honors those who honor their parents.

I knew an old man, I worked for him. I saw this in his life. As a young man during the depression, his parents were going to lose their farm to back taxes. He went to work in a CCC camp in Upper Michigan, to pay their taxes. It was terrible hard work, but he did it. He saved his parents farm. His parents did not even leave their farm to him; they left it to another brother. God honored him anyway; my friend had one of the most beautiful farms I had ever seen. He was very blessed. He lived long too. God honors His word when we obey it.

All through scripture we see God using families. Families are to look out for each other. Our family is our ministry to God. God does things in households. Noah brought his family into the ark, in Genesis 7:1 *Then the Lord said to Noah, "Come into the ark, you and all your household, because*

I have seen that you are righteous before Me in this generation." Noah's ark was his family's salvation.

Rahab the harlot's entire family was saved out of Jericho because of her kindness to the two Hebrew spies. Not just Rahab but her father and mother and all their children and all that belonged to them. That included nieces and nephews; they all were saved because of Rahab. She didn't just plead for herself but for her entire family. *Joshua 6:17 "Now the city shall be doomed by the Lord to destruction, it and all who are in it. Only Rahab the harlot shall live, she and all who are in the house, because she hid the messengers that we sent."* Rahab's actions saved not only herself but her entire family.

The book of Genesis records the amazing story of Joseph. He was sold into slavery by his jealous brothers, but this was God's plan to save the entire family of Jacob from the famine that was to come. Joseph goes from slavery to prison and then to ruler over all of Egypt, second only to the Pharaoh. Joseph was put in this situation to SAVE his entire family, even the brothers that sold him to slavery and even their wives and children, every single family member.

Are you starting to get my point? Our families <u>are</u> our business. God has families to help one another. So, no one falls through the cracks. So, the important jobs get done. If someone dies there is someone else to raise the children that are left. When someone falls down there is someone to pick them up. And hopefully because of our righteousness we can bring our families through trials like Noah and Rahab and Joseph.

What can I do for God? I can start right at home; I can love and care for my mate. I can raise my children to know Him. I can honor my parents. I can realize that God loves families even extended family, and this is holy ground. How I treat my family is very important to God.

But if anyone does not provide for his own, and especially for those of his household, he has denied the faith and is worse than an unbeliever. 1 Timothy 5:8

Chapter Eight
Faithful in the Small Things

He who is faithful in what is least is faithful also in much; and he who is unjust in what is least is also unjust in what is much. Luke 16:10

We need to have the heart of a servant toward our Lord. We need to do what He tells us to and not judge the importance, just obey.

How can we possibly know the value of what He is doing when He gives us a command? A small thing may have big consequences or big thing may have small consequences. Only God sees the whole picture, we have to trust Him and obey Him. If you are called to work in the nursery or to preach before millions, what is that to you, be faithful.

The Bible says… *"Or which of you having a servant plowing or tending sheep, will say to him when he has come in from tending the field, 'Come at once and sit down to eat'? But will he not rather say to him, 'Prepare something for my supper, and gird yourself and serve me till I have eaten and drunk, and afterward you will eat and drink'? Does he thank that servant because he did the things that were commanded him? I think not. So likewise, you, when you have done all those things which are commanded, say, "We are unprofitable servants we have done what was our duty to do.'"* Luke 17:7-10

God may ask you to write a book or write a letter, be faithful the outcome is God's plan, your part is to do what He asks.

Giving Your All

I remember hearing a visiting evangelist in our church tell us a story about when he was first starting out in the ministry. He showed up to preach at a meeting and there were only five people present. He said that God had sent him there, so even though the place was almost empty, he poured out his heart and preached his very best. After his sermon one young boy came forward in the altar call. After hearing the sermon, he felt called to preach.   Now years later just a few miles from the place the evangelist preached that sermon is a very large church. The pastor of the big church is the young man that was present in the meeting all those years ago. The one who came forward for prayer and felt the call to preach.

Every time this evangelist drives down this road and sees this large thriving church, he knows it started the night he preached his heart out to five people. That church was birthed that night. He wasn't discouraged because there was no crowd! He was faithful in the small things!

I read a similar story that is also true. I read it in a biography of a man who is a great evangelist and is also Jewish. In his book he told of a woman he knew, God told her He was leading her to the Jewish people. How did God send her to the Jewish people? God told her to get a job at a Jewish orphanage. She did and while she worked there, she led one troubled young Jewish orphan to Jesus. The young man became a great evangelist with a worldwide ministry. She was faithful in the small things. Her faithfulness was part of God's plan to start a worldwide ministry.

Summer is Helped by Strangers

Little things can make big differences. A smile, a kind word or a helping hand can make a difference in someone's life.

There was a particular time in my life which was so difficult I didn't think I was going to make it through. My husband and I were walking through the valley of the shadow of death. But in the middle of this time of trial, we received three acts of kindness from total strangers that gave us hope.

During this time, I was pregnant with my third child, Joy. My husband was only getting a little work here and there through a union hall. We didn't have enough money to live on and we were having a trial with a close family member who was in trouble. We were barely eating; we had been asked to leave our apartment and had nowhere to go and things just kept getting worse. Our only vehicle kept breaking down and every time we got a little money it went to getting it fixed. The mechanic told us we needed tires, but we had no money. On top of everything else it was Christmas time and we had nothing for our children.

One day I got a little work helping an elderly lady at her home and thought I was going to have a little money to buy food. Not so, because that same day my husband was in our van and two tires blew out at the same time.

It caused a small accident. Jim was arrested for the accident, and our vehicle was impounded. Jim was given a court date and told if he wanted our vehicle back, he had to be at the impound lot the following morning by eight am with fifty dollars and if he was late the fee would go up to one hundred dollars.

We managed to scrape up the fifty dollars, but we didn't have another penny. Jim could not get anyone to drive him to the impound lot, so he took off hitch hiking. Jim was desperate to get there on time so we wouldn't lose our vehicle, an old dilapidated van.

Act of kindness number one was from the man who picked Jim up hitchhiking. He was a retired police officer, he rushed Jim straight to the impound lot. They were late and the lot wouldn't give Jim our van back, they wanted one hundred dollars now.

This man went in and convinced them to give Jim a break. Jim had no way to drive the van because it was missing two tires. This man called a tire man who came with two used tires and told us to pay when we could.

I don't know who this man was that helped us that day but some twenty-five years later I still think of him with gratitude. He was our Good Samaritan. We were at a point where we couldn't help ourselves and this stranger stopped and helped us. God bless him!!!

The second act of kindness happened a few days later. I was at the Salvation Army office waiting in the outer office for some food. I was sitting there with my little girl Lonna; she was three and a half years old.

Lonna was born loving clothes. As soon as she could walk, she would constantly get into her clothes. I didn't have a dresser for her, I used a garment bag that hung up in the closet and had cardboard shelves. She would get into that garment bag and put on one outfit on top of another. She was obsessed with her clothes. Of course, we didn't have money for new clothes, so she wore hand me downs.

So, the two of us were sitting in the outer office of the Salvation Army when a woman came in with two big garbage bags that were tied shut. I think she came in to donate the contents of the bags, but she saw us and changed her mind. She looked at Lonna and I sitting there and said, "These are for you," handed us the bags and left.

We got home and opened the bags and there were thirty of the most beautiful dresses I had ever seen in my life. They were Lonna's size and one size up too. Most of the dresses were Polly Flinders, the kind with smocking and ruffles.

Here we were living in incredible poverty wondering if we were going to be homeless and my daughter was dressed like a princess. It was like a light in the darkness that gave me hope, another act of kindness by a complete stranger.

The third act of kindness was to come. A friend called me and said, "Someone brought you something and left it at my house." I went and there were many bags of groceries, and in the groceries was even a big jar of Tums and a package of Q tips! Two things I had been without for months.

Whoever gave us all these things had even bought me a maternity outfit that was beautiful; I wore it for the rest of my pregnancy. I never found out who gave us all those groceries.

That was the darkest time of my entire life and I have been through many trials, but that period was the hardest, {well one of the hardest}. Three complete strangers and their acts of kindness gave us hope and kept us from total despair. I am so glad they were faithful!

Faithful in Small Things

When I was young and in my early twenties, I longed to write. I would sit with a pen and paper in my hands and stare at the paper. It was just itching in me to write a story or a book or SOMETHING!

I told the Lord I wanted to write. He told me to write a letter.

I wrote letters to a couple of people that God directed me to and told them about the Lord. It wasn't exactly what I had in mind, but I was faithful. I thought that was the end of my writing career.

It was more than twenty-five years later the Lord told me to write a book. By that time, it surprised me because I knew I didn't know how to write a book.

If I can be faithful with what the Lord wants to say in a letter, I guess I can be faithful with what He wants me to say in a book.

I just now received a call from the principal of my grandson, David's, school; Mr. Jones. David is in kindergarten, which is a miracle that he is in regular school. David started school the month before he turned three because he didn't speak. Because of his lack of speech sometimes he gets very upset and hard to handle.

The principal called me to tell me that David was upset and wouldn't get off the bus because he didn't have his backpack or his special car he loves and wanted for show and tell. The principal came and got David off the bus and promised to try to get him his car. That is when he called me.

Tears came to my eyes. "Thank you, God for a principle who is faithful in the small things, the things that are important to kindergarteners."

I found the car and the backpack and brought them to school. I know my grandson is in good hands because Mr. Jones the principal is faithful in the small things.

I want to be faithful in the small things. If we are, God will give us more. Maybe God is so interested in small things because of His great love for us. He loves us so and He cares about every detail of our lives. The Bible says even the hairs of our head are numbered.

What can I do for God?

I can be faithful in everything He gives me to do, even the small things.

Chapter Nine
Pay Your Bills

Owe no one anything except to love one another, for he who loves one another has fulfilled the law. Romans 13:8

I want you to know why I am writing this chapter. It was a total surprise to me; in fact, I am writing this last even later than the last chapter, I am just putting it here in the middle.

I am writing it because; I have been troubled by the attitude of young people toward finances. I have seen young mothers that say they don't have money for diapers that are holding a Starbucks coffee and smoking a cigarette. I have seen young people eating at Applebee's or some other restaurant, when they have bills that are going unpaid. I even had a family member receive a huge tax refund of several thousand dollars and only weeks later got an eviction notice, she didn't pay her bills. I have seen young couples that owe money and have young children with many needs buy large screen televisions. It troubles me that we have a generation that has their priorities so mixed up. This is wrong and it is unpleasing to God!

The Problem of Greed

I am also troubled by the greed I see in this country. Companies are no longer motivated by offering something beneficial to the public; they are motivated by greed. Profit comes first, even if it means harming the public. Food companies add harmful ingredients because they are cheaper. Every kind of scam you can imagine is out there, just to get your money.

And then I was surfing the internet one day. I was going to different Christian web sites and reading testimonies. I ran across one of those sites where people have had supernatural revelations of Heaven or Hell.

I love those kinds of testimonies. This one I had never read before. It told of someone's visit to Hell with Jesus, I had read many like this, but this one was a little different, the person saw a place in hell for people who did not pay their bills.

It terrified me and I quickly clicked off that site. I did not like that, and I did not want to believe it, and I am not even saying that I do believe it, but it started me thinking.

I believe this problem originates from greed. Greed seems to be the sin of our time. People run up bills they cannot pay and then they just file for bankruptcy, leaving everyone in their wake financially hurt.

And corporation heads give themselves huge bonuses while their employees can't even make enough to live on.

Then there are many investment companies that have squandered the life savings of their investors, they are on the news in alarming rates, it is an epidemic.

And our young people think they have to have everything to get started and buy, buy, buy more than they can pay for. We need to live within our means!

I remember seeing a young engaged couple on an afternoon talk show. The young bride to be wanted a big fancy wedding she couldn't afford. The wedding she was planning cost twenty thousand dollars! They were going to put it on a credit card. The young groom did not want to do it.

They brought in a financial counselor to help them decide. The young bride thought she deserved a big wedding; after all it was her big day. I can't believe how ridiculous that is!!!! To spend a fortune, you don't have, on one day!

Doing the Golden Rule

Why is it so important as a Christian to pay our bills? I believe it comes down to the golden rule. *Therefore, whatever you want men to do to you, do also to them, for this is the Law and the prophets. Matthew 7:12.*

This attitude of greed in our nation, and among the young people, the lack of integrity or we could even call it irresponsibility, is totally the opposite of the example of Christ. We need to value others as ourselves. That means we don't see them as a means for us to get what we want.

We need to see this from God's perspective. God has a plan for everyone's life, and that plan includes their provision. When someone because of greediness doesn't pay a person what they owe them or over charges them or somehow takes their provision, God is involved. He sees it as His responsibility to supply their need. Now you have violated Him. It is like stealing.

I learned this lesson once. It was a time when I had left my husband for several months and was staying at a little efficiency apartment at a small hotel with my three small children. {I wrote a whole chapter on this time, in my first book *The Impossible Marriage.*} The rent for the efficiency was three hundred dollars a month. I had to go on assistance for a couple of months at this time.

When the hotel owner filled out my assistance papers, he raised the rent because he figured if the government was paying, he ought to get a little more, so he upped the rent thirty dollars. This meant I got less, and I was thirty dollars short every month. I didn't have enough to go to the laundry mat.

I didn't think too much about it until the Lord spoke to me about it. He asked me to pray for the man.

"I don't need to pray for him Lord." I told Him "It doesn't bother me at all. I have managed to get along."

Someone had come by and given one of my kids some money for their birthday and I used it for laundry that month.

The Lord showed me it bothered Him and why. He had planned for my every need during this time. Then He showed told me this also. "When I look at you, I don't see time. I see your whole life and everything about you from beginning to end. I see this man's sin every time I look at you. Will pray for him?" So, I prayed and asked God to forgive the man.

We need to treat others with great respect because they are God's business. Their provision is His business, and we need to pay them if we owe them and not cheat them.

Respect for the Hard Work of Others

One person I have respected financially is my husband. There were many years he worked very hard so I could stay home with our children. When he would hand me the money every week, I treated every penny like a drop of his blood, because I knew how hard he worked to get it.

I studied the grocery ads with a plan to save every penny I could. I never splurged on myself or spent recklessly, I couldn't.

I remember one time my husband was working as a waiter, and he broke his foot. He had a cast and was supposed to be off his foot for quite a while. The only problem was after two weeks we were totally out of money; he had to go back to work.

When he went back to work the manager told him you can't come to work and wait on tables with that cast on. So, my husband went in the back and cut his cast off and worked in pain on a broken foot.

There were many times he did things like that to provide. One time he was working construction on a new hotel. It was the only job he could find.

He came home and told me. "Three guys walked off the job today. They wanted them to work on a scaffolding ten stories high and they wouldn't do it."

"Oh," I said thinking it wasn't worth any amount of money to do that, then asked, "Who did they get to do it?"

"I did it." Jim replied.

How could I waste a penny of the money he earned?

I couldn't.

I feel this way about others too. I have never sold a car of mine for more than junk price because I have never wanted to rip anyone off. If I thought a car was no good, I would junk it myself and not sell it to anyone.

I remember one time I sold an old Pontiac we had passed around through the family, first my daughter drove it then I drove it, then my youngest daughter drove it.

When my youngest daughter bought a better car, I asked the mechanic about the old Pontiac. He told me the engine was good and would probably go another hundred thousand miles.

So, I decided to sell it for three hundred dollars. A young man and his father came to buy it. He had just gotten his driver's license and his dad was teaching him how to buy a car. The young man paid me then he looked me in the eye, while his proud father watched, and shook my hand. I was happy to be a little part of the young man's life, the lady that sold him his first car. It was a good car, and I knew it. We need to respect others money and work.

Do the Best You Can

My husband and I have lived on very little income through the years. That means we have spent very little. We have never bought a new car, not even close to new. We have never bought a new piece of furniture. We have always tried to keep up with our bills.

There were a few times my husband did not have work or had very little. During those times we had to set priorities with the little money we had. The first priority was something to eat. I worded it like that because in those times you eat as cheap as possible.

The second priority was to keep a roof over our head. After all your immediate needs to live, {and that means needs not wants} you pay your bills. If you don't waste money and you still get behind on your bills, which has happened to us too, {I owed the doctor for years, but I eventually paid him off,} try to work on your bills when you can, God will help you, be sure to ask Him and then use the money He provides wisely and be responsible. Remember paying bills comes before luxuries like eating out or going to movies or on trips or buying anything new.

I have to admit I had to pay a couple of bills before I wrote this chapter. I had two surgeries several months ago and the bills have been rolling in ever since. We had kept up with them at first, but we ran out of money. Several bills went to collections. I had to pay them before I could write this chapter. I have been taking overtime when my job offers it to try to catch up.

There have been times I have gotten bills I thought were unfair and decided not to pay. I remember one time I got a bill from chiropractor that Jim and the kids had been to over a year before. I wondered why I got a bill because it was one hundred percent covered by our health insurance. I called the insurance company to ask them about it. They said it would have been covered if the chiropractor's office would have submitted the bill earlier, they had a year limitation.

Apparently, the office had an incompetent person doing their billing, they fired her and went over the books and found her mistakes, so I was getting billed over a year later and now it wasn't covered.

I should have never prayed about it because I thought I had a pretty good excuse not to pay, but when I prayed about it the Lord said, "Just pay it."

So, I paid it. I have to say the Lord provided the money though, I didn't think I could swing but I did. Apparently, it was important to the Lord that I pay that bill.

Over the years I have been so tight with money that a few times the Lord would speak to me and tell me to spend on something. Like the time He told me to buy a pool.

I love to swim. Sam's Club had a sixteen foot by four-foot swimming pool on sale in their store for two hundred and ninety-nine dollars. The Lord told me to buy it. {I had to buy it the Lord told me to.} I didn't think I could afford it but obviously I could. That pool lasted for six summers, my grandchildren and I loved every minute, splashing and having fun. Last summer I knew was the last summer for that pool, it was really worn out. The price of the pool went up since I bought the first one and I knew for sure I could not afford new one.

I prayed about it, I told the Lord I wanted the very same pool because I know how to put that one up and I know how to run it. A couple of weeks later I went to a garage sale and there was my pool. It was the exact same pool, the people had bought it and put it up, but their kids never swam in it, so they decided to sell it. It was in perfect condition. I paid forty-five dollars for a new pool, and not only did I get the pool I got all their chemicals too, and just the chemicals cost more than forty-five dollars.

God wants us to have nice things, but He doesn't want us to get in financial trouble over things. If you feel you have so many bills that you will never get them paid off, I don't want you to despair. I believe if you are faithful to try, God will come to your aid.

I recently heard a missionary speak. He told about how he and his wife felt called to become missionaries, but they couldn't because he was eighty thousand dollars in debt from his student loans from college! They felt they would never get to go. He thought it would take a lifetime to get out of debt. He started praying and paying.

Soon his wife was hired for an extremely high paying job at a huge factory. He was able to pay his student loans in just a couple of years and then go on the mission field. He is still there today. If you decide to do the right thing God will help you.

We are learning about pleasing God by paying our bills. It is fulfilling the golden rule, to love others as we love ourselves. We want to respect others and not overcharge them if we sell them something or cheat them in any way.

We want to have good priorities in the way we spend our money and take care of our responsibilities.

We want to please God by being different from those in the world who are motivated by greed. We need to be motivated by love and respect and treat others the way we want to be treated.

Chapter Ten
Pressing into God

Trust in the Lord and do good; Dwell in the land and feed on His faithfulness. Delight yourself also in the Lord, and He shall give you the desires of your heart. Psalms 37:3-4

Pressing into God is a win, win situation. It is a win, win, win, win situation. What do I mean by pressing into God? I mean getting closer to God, focusing on Him, spending time with Him. Who wins? You win and everyone around you wins.

I remember one time a new lady started at work; her name was Patty. She had recently beaten a drug habit with the Lord's help. She was excited about the Lord! Every day was packed with excitement for her. She was in love with the Lord. Every day she would come into work excited and want me to listen to what the Lord told her in her prayer time that day. She was telling me wonderful things.

I was jealous! I wanted to hear from God like she was. I remembered I used to be as excited as she was. I wanted that again. She lit a fire under me, out of jealousy, {good jealousy}. I started getting excited about God again too. I started spending more time with Him again, praying more and reading my Bible more. I started hearing from God again too. I needed the boost she gave me.

The Bible says: *Oh, taste and see that the Lord is good Psalms 34:8.* Sometimes we forget what He tastes like. We forget how delicious He is. We need to taste again.

Pressing into God is great for us, and it is great for those around us. Do you have family members you have been worried about because you feel they have been drifting away from the Lord? You don't need to preach at them. When you get close to God, and you press into Him; you are drawing them to Him.

There is nothing more enticing than God's presence; if you have God, others will want Him too.

Most people are not led to the Lord so much by what people say as by seeing Christ in them. Yes, we need to speak up too, but if they see nothing different in your life than theirs, what you say will not be effective. Living close to the Lord will show others the truth. That is one win. Yes, it is important to speak about our faith, but two thirds are the living it, showing others the truth.

Carol's Conversations about God

Let's talk about God for a while. It will take us millions of years or longer to get to know Him, to see how good He is and all the aspects of His being. My sister, Carol calls me all the time just to talk about God. She studies Quantum Physics for a hobby. It gets her all excited because Quantum Physics shows her more about God. She calls me all excited and tells me things I have trouble bending my mind around. She recently called me with one of these conversations.

"Summer," she cried, "There is a secret to our universe. The secret is Jesus!"

I couldn't wait to hear where this was going. She continued.

"One Quantum Physicist believes we are living in a hologram. Our world is only a shadow of an invisible world. Everything is made up of energy that is only visible when someone looks at it."

She paused a moment to let that sink in. Then she went

on.

"Everything we see, every star or mountain or tree, everything that is visible came out of the thoughts of God. It started in His thoughts. Then He spoke it forth and everything was created out of His faith. So, what is more real?" she asked me, "What is created or the faith that it is created from?"

"I don't know." I answered her.

"The faith is more real. We are literally God's thoughts that have taken on a life of our own. *Ephesians 1:4 says just as he chose us in Him before the foundation of the world, that we should be holy and without blame before Him in love.* Where were we before the foundation of the world?"

She didn't wait for an answer.

"We existed in the mind of God we were part of His thoughts, but now we have taken on a life of our own. Remember," she reminded me, "That movie we saw, the story of the girl with the imaginary friend, her imaginary friend existed in her mind, but then at the end of the movie he takes on a life of his own."

It was a cute romance movie we had seen; the story was about a young girl whose mother is very domineering and does not let the daughter be who she really is. The daughter in her childhood creates an imaginary friend who helps her deal with her mother's control. When she grows up egged on by her mother, she is about to marry a man who dominates her like her mother did. This is when her imaginary friend reappears to help her again. She falls in love with her imaginary friend, and she breaks off with her controlling fiancé. Then at the end her imaginary friend becomes a real man. He takes on a life of his own.

"We are like that movie," she continued," We have come from God's imagination and taken on a life of our own. We are literally a part of God; we are His thoughts come to life."

Have I lost you yet? This is a typical conversation with my sister. She is excited about God! She is always looking for someone to talk about Him to. She is always blowing my mind with what she has learned. It is exciting! Pressing into God is exciting!

Spending Time with the Trinity

I remember a teaching I heard years ago. An evangelist came to our church when I was in high school; I still remember his sermon all these years later. He talked about getting to know God, each of the Trinity. He said he could tell which one of the Trinity a person had been spending time with by their conversation.

He said if someone was spending time with the Father they would be talking about love. If they said something like, "God is so loving, it is all about love." Then the evangelist knew they had been keeping company with the Father, because love is His nature.

If they were talking about wisdom, they had been spending time with Jesus. Jesus is the Word. He reminded us in the Bible of how many times the Pharisees sent people with trick questions to trip Jesus up so they could accuse Him of false teaching but every time, He answered them so well, the people were amazed.

Like the time they asked Him about paying taxes to Caesar, and Jesus told them to give to Caesar what belongs to Caesar and give to God what belongs to God.

Or like the time they asked Him about in whose authority He had come. Jesus response was the question about John baptism "Was it from God or from men?" They couldn't answer because if they said from God, then Jesus would say, "Then why didn't you believe him?" And if they said from men the people would stone them because they esteemed him a prophet from God.

Jesus stumped them every time. He has perfect wisdom. He is also able to solve our problems with perfect wisdom if we seek Him. So, the evangelist told us if he heard someone talking about the wisdom of God, they had been spending time with Jesus.

The evangelist went on to tell us if people were talking about the power of God, they had been spending time with the Holy Spirit. The Holy Spirit is the power of God. He is the one that is here with us on earth. He is the one that knocks people over in prayer lines, causes people to dance or run or cry or laugh hysterically or puts people in trances and they see visions.

If you have no idea what I am talking about, get to some good Holy Ghost revivals. I have been in many and have experienced some of these things. The Holy Spirit is lively, that is for sure.

Of course, that is just the beginning of getting to know God. I have learned to distinguish the three different voices of God. They are also discussed in scripture. The Father's voice is booming, like thunder, or the ocean. He shakes you to your socks.

Jesus voice is so familiar, like it is a part of you. Like you have known it all your life, you just didn't pay attention. I don't know how else to describe it except to say it is a familiar voice. And the Holy Spirit's voice is best described as a still small voice. It is easy to dismiss if you don't train yourself to hear it or if you are distracted by the world.

The Secret Place

Pressing into God fills us up. We can't pour out to others if we haven't filled up. Do you want more good in your life, fill up with God. God is everything good in our universe. He is the source of light, of love, of joy and of peace. The Bible says in *James 1:17 Every perfect gift is from above, and comes down from the Father of lights, with whom there is no variation or shadow of turning.* As we press into God, we get more light and love and joy and peace.

There are places in the Bible that talk about the secret place. It is mentioned in *Psalms 91:1 He that dwells in the secret place of the Most High shall abide under the shadow of the Almighty.*

The secret place is a wonderful place, those who dwell

there are safe. Psalms 91 goes on to tell us, secret place dwellers, that a thousand may fall at our side and ten thousand at our right hand but it will not come near us, only with our eyes will we see the reward of the wicked.

Psalms 3:20 also mentions the secret place. *You shall hide them in the secret place of Your presence from the plots of man, you shall keep them secretly in a pavilion from the strife of tongues.* No one can hurt you in the secret place.

Psalms 27:5 says, *For in the time of trouble, He shall hide me in His pavilion, In the secret place of His tabernacle he shall hide me; He shall set me high upon a rock.*

Would you like to be in God's secret place? It is up to you. God is willing. I have had people tell me God doesn't like them. That is ridiculous. You can be as close to God as <u>YOU</u> want to be. The Bible says, *Draw near to God and He <u>will</u> draw near to you. James 4:8*

If you draw closer to God, He will draw closer to you!!!! Another win!

I am learning that getting closer to God is up to me. If I get closer to Him, He will get closer to me.

I can't pour out to others unless I am filled up myself. Pressing into God benefits me, and it benefits those around me. They will want what I have.

The more I press into God the more good things will be in my life, like peace, joy and love. The more I press into God the safer I will be.

Pressing into God is a win, win, win situation!

Chapter Eleven
No Age Requirements

Assuredly I say to you, unless you are converted and become as little children, you will by no means enter the kingdom of heaven. Therefore, whoever humbles himself as this little child is the greatest in the kingdom of heaven. And whoever receives one little child like this in my name receives Me. Matthew 18:3-5

The things that are important to God are not confined to things like age limits, gender or race. Children, many times are very receptive to God, and they definitely can be used by Him.

Samuel was called by God at a very young age. John the Baptist leapt in his mother's womb when he heard the voice of Mary, the Lord's mother. Spiritual things are understood by the spirit! They are not understood by intellect. John the Baptist an infant in his mother's womb spiritually discerned the voice of Mary, the presence of the Lord within her and his spirit leapt for joy!

Children Can Serve the Lord

I remember thinking, when my first child was very

small, that he needed to wait until he was older to become a Christian so that it would mean something to him. I was wrong. One day while my three-year-old son, Jamie was at my sister's house, he accepted the Lord into his heart. They were reading a Christian story book together and when they finished, Jamie said to his aunt, "I want to ask Jesus into my heart."

So, they prayed together. I immediately noticed the change in his personality. He was clingy and scared before and now he was trusting the Lord! Soon after he started to tell me he wanted to speak in tongues.

"No, you're too young," I told him. I didn't think someone so young could have that experience.

He persisted. Finally, I told him, "We will leave it up to the Lord. You can ask Him; we will see what He does."

That seemed to satisfy Jamie. A couple days later he was speaking in tongues! He was so excited he was telling everyone, "I can speak in tongues!" then he'd start showing them. Not only was he speaking in tongues his little sister Lonna was speaking in tongues and she didn't talk yet.

Lonna was three also when she accepted Jesus. I picked her up from the nursery one Sunday and the teacher told me, "Lonna prayed and asked Jesus into her heart today."

When my third child Joy Belle came along Jamie was six and Lonna was three almost four. When we brought Joy home from the hospital, Jamie and Lonna said, "We can't wait until Joy is old enough to talk, so we can lead her to Jesus."

Joy can't remember when she got saved because Jamie and Lonna knelt her down and prayed with her so many times when she was tiny; she is not quite sure when it happened.

God uses children, even little children. When Jamie was about three years old, I was sitting in the church hallway with him and the other mothers. We had a section in the hall at church where we could see into the service but sit with small children. Jamie and I were sitting there when a friend of mine came up. She was upset because she was supposed to sing the special music for the church, but she had laryngitis and could only whisper. Three-year-old Jamie laid hands on her throat and asked Jesus to heal her. Instantly she could speak; we were both surprised. She got up and sang for the church and had no trouble at all with her voice. Children have great faith!

Several years later Jamie prayed for me too, and I was instantly healed. I had never had any pets as a child because my mother had a severe allergy to animals. When I got older, I realized I had the same problem. Jim had brought a dog home for the kids, and I was so miserable, I didn't think we would be able to keep him. My eyes were swollen and itchy, I felt awful. I felt bad because the kids had bonded to the dog.

"What's wrong, mom?" Jamie asked me, seeing the worried look on my face.

"I am allergic to the dog, and I don't think we can keep him. I feel bad about it." I told him.

Jamie just smiled like that is easy to fix, no problem, laid his hands on me and prayed. Instantly I felt a gush of water in my eyes, then I felt fine. I have never been allergic to dogs or cats since. {We have had many of both.} It was an instant lasting healing. Children have such uncomplicated faith.

Many people don't realize children can be strong Christians. At church we had a monthly service for communion. The pastor that officiated the communion service asked that we did not let our small children partake of the bread and juice. So, I did not let Joy, who was two at the time, take any. The next month at the communion service the pastor said the same thing. As the communion plates came toward me the Lord spoke to me. "Last month you obeyed man," He told me, "This month obey Me. I want Joy to take communion." I never stopped Joy from taking communion again.

My children when they were little have prayed, prophesied and seen visions. Jesus said let the children come to Him. Little people can be very strong spiritually. Being used by God has no age limits.

We Need the Elderly

What about the elderly? What can they do for God? Prayer is such an amazing and powerful thing. From your chair in your living room, you can reach around the globe in prayer and change the world! It only takes faith; it doesn't take muscle or money or physical strength.

Prayer can protect those in danger, heal those who are sick, encourage the hopeless, change nations and even raise the dead. Yes, we need the prayers of older Christians. Grandfathers and grandmothers don't stop praying for your grandchildren.

A Grandmothers Prayers

I read an amazing story of how a grandmother's prayers saved her grandson from hell.

This young man was raised in a Christian home, but he rebelled. At eighteen he moved in with four other boys and they spent their time doing drugs. Their house became a drug house.

One night they got a whole cache of different drugs and this young man passed out and died. He woke up stone cold sober standing before God. His life was played before him like a video tape, everything he ever did. Every sin he ever committed he watched replayed.

At the end, because he had never accepted Jesus as his Savior, he was pronounced guilty and sentenced to hell. As he descended into torment he screamed to God for mercy.

Jesus appeared and started pulling the young man out of hell. Then Satan appeared and like a lawyer in a courtroom, he had a case put together against this young man why he should go to hell. The young man went through what he described as being, like a tug of war between the devil and Jesus.

Finally, Jesus said to the young man, "I am saving you because of the prayers of your grandmother, she has prayed for you continually."

The tug of war ended, and the Lord sent the young man

back to earth. He woke up in the drug house alive again! He immediately left the drug house and drove home.

From that night on he was changed. He never took another drug; he gave his heart to the Lord and entered the mission field. His grandmother's prayers saved him from an eternity in torment. He thought it was hopeless. He thought he was lost and doomed forever, but God honored his grandmother's continual prayers. He literally pulled him out of hell, just because of her!

This astounds me! It also inspires me, to pray for my children and grandchildren continually.

Yes, we need the prayers of the elderly, we need their wisdom too. They have already been through the seasons of life we are about to face and can help us as we go through them also.

There are no age requirements in the spirit. I will never forget one time when my son was very little, he was laying on my bed, sound asleep, it was late. My husband, Jim was sitting on the side of the bed, his head in his hands.

My husband has struggled with his own salvation all his life. He was feeling despair. "It's useless," my husband cried, "God doesn't love me!"

Little Jamie never appeared to wake up and he never opened his little eyes, but to our amazement, he chirped in his little voice, "Jesus love you daddy. He really do."

My husband's mouth dropped open in amazement. The wisdom of a child ministered to him. Children are very precious to God. They have faith that is big. We can learn from them as we teach them. We need the elderly too. We can glean from their many years of experience. There are no age limits to be used by God because God is contacted by our spirit, not our intellect. Our spirits are eternal, they are ageless.

Chapter Twelve
I Go to Church

And let us consider one another in order to stir up love and good works, not forsaking the assembling of ourselves together, as is the manner of some, but exhorting one another, and so much more as you see the day approaching. Hebrews 10:24-24

There are spiritual reasons why you should belong to and attend church. It should be a Bible believing church that preaches salvation in the blood of Jesus.

We are in an invisible war, an invisible, spiritual war with real enemies. Your church is protection. It is your regiment of soldiers. Your fellow church members are your marching partners against the enemy.

Is it any wonder Satan attacks churches so? The enemy would like to draw you off alone so you will be an easier to ensnare in some trap.

The Benefits of Your Church

I did not realize this at first, but the Lord taught me a few things. At our church we had several families that needed houses. Jim and I were trying to buy a house too. We lived in a mobile home at the time, but the Lord had told us to buy a big house. We met so much spiritual opposition every time we got close to getting a house something would happen. My husband lost his job, or some other financial difficulty would happen and once they sold the house we were buying out from under us to another couple.

We just couldn't make it happen. There were several other families in our church trying to get a house. One family was homeless. Finally, we got our house. It was so quick and such a miracle I couldn't believe it. We looked at the house and several weeks later we owned it.

The same month we got our house the other families in the church finally got places too, even the homeless family. The Lord showed me this was no coincidence. We were connected together spiritually, and once one of us broke through the enemy lines we all got through together. There is strength in numbers!

The Lord showed me more. Sometimes when someone was up in front at church for prayer, I would not join in. I thought I can't pray for them, I have too many problems of my own. While the church was praying, I might get bored or let my mind wander or even worse yet be jealous that everyone was praying for them when I felt I needed it worse.

The Lord showed me to get in there and pray with the rest of them. We are all joined together, even if we are praying for sister Sally's arthritis, we all are breaking through the enemy's lines with our prayers. If we all join in, it is like a platoon with a battering ram pounding on the enemy's gates. When we break through the enemy lines, we can all take the spoils! When we break through, that is when we can reach in with the arm of faith and take what we need. There is an open Heaven and a time for prayer to be answered.

This sure changed my attitude, when someone else is up at front for prayer I add my prayers, I want us to break through the enemy lines together.

Church and union with the body of Christ will also provide us with spiritual protection. The Bible says one can put a thousand to flight and two can put ten thousand to flight.

And there are some very practical reasons to go to church. In hard times I have received help from the people of my church. When I had a baby, they brought us meals. One man from our church paid our rent when we got behind. Most churches have counseling, food pantries; some have emergency funds to help with bigger needs. Churches also help with funerals and weddings. And there are also the fun things like church picnics, potluck dinners, camps, some have baseball teams and other sports. Churches provide many needs.

One time when I was helping a ministry that worked with the homeless, I met a man there who was destitute. He told me he was a Christian, but he was down and out and couldn't seem to get back on his feet. He was homeless and living in the park and often went without food.

I told him, "Your Christian brothers and sisters would help you if they knew you. You need to pick a church and go every Sunday. When people get to know you and what is happening in your life, they will help you."

Several months later this man came to find me in the park on a Sunday afternoon. He told me he took my advice. He had begun regularly attending church and he told me what church he was going to; I was pleased because I knew it was a good church. He was making friends. He told me the people there were helping him get back on his feet. He was very happy. Church provides us spiritual support, physical support and emotional support.

Tithing

I also want to talk about tithing in this chapter. If you are thinking I cannot tithe because I can't get my bills paid as it is; I have been there too. I had stopped tithing because I was so broke. I gave here and there.

God helped me get back on track. I was going to a wonderful little church in a storefront at the time. The pastor's wife got up and talked about tithing. She said, "We are going to start with a penny. We are going to pass the collection plate and if you are not tithing start with a penny."

I put my penny in. That night while I was delivering newspapers on my paper route, about four thirty in the morning a customer was waiting for me with a ten-dollar tip. That had never happened to me before. The next offering, I put in my ten-dollar tip.

From that point on I stepped out in faith and started putting in one hundred dollars a month, which was about ten percent of what I earned. I found my bills were getting paid, so I raised it. I have been tithing ever since.

From that time on my finances seemed to improve. I think it is important that the church you tithe to is preaching the gospel. I want to see others getting saved. I also like to send money to ministries I think are really reaching the lost.

Tithing is important. It is how the body of Christ operates on this earth. It also comes with a promise, that God will rebuke the devourer on our behalf. Tithing partners us with God in our finances. It puts us in a place of faith in the financial area.

I also feel God has shown me it will be extremely important in the days to come to be tithing. That the world's financial systems will be crumbling. We need to have our bank accounts with God kept up to date. We need our faith and hope to be in God's kingdom, and it will be if we are walking in faith and obedience with our finances.

What can I do for God? I can obey his word about attending church. This protects me from the evil one. I can pray fervently for the needs of those in my church and we will break through together, and when we do, I will reach in with the arm of faith and get my needs met also. I can help finance the Kingdom of God with my tithes and offerings, and my finances will become God's business. God wants me to do these things so I will have protection and be blessed!

Chapter Thirteen
I Love My Country

Therefore, I exhort first of all that supplications, prayers, intercessions, and giving of thanks be made for all men, for kings and all who are in authority, that we may lead a quiet and peaceable life in all godliness and reverence. For this is good and acceptable in the sight of God our Savior, who desires all men to be saved and come to the knowledge of the truth. Timothy 2: 1-4

The body of Christ, that is me and you, we have a responsibility to our country. We have the responsibility to pray, vote, to stand up for what is right and to take a stand against evil. First of all, the Bible commands us to pray for our leaders. Do not worry about praying for ungodly leaders; we can pray that God will change their hearts and lead them.

All the strange weather and disasters and horrible things we have been seeing are a result of sin. Sin causes a reaction in nature. If the body of Christ prays for this country, good changes will come. God's word promises it.

"When I shut up heaven and there is no rain or command the locusts to devour the land, or send pestilence among My people, if My people who are called by My name will humble themselves, and pray and seek My face and turn from

their wicked ways, then I will hear from Heaven, forgive their sin and heal their land. 2 Chronicles 7: 13-14

We also have a responsibility to vote and vote righteously. I am talking about protecting the unborn. Any candidate that does not respect the life of an unborn child will not respect life in general. If you disrespect life, you also disrespect the Creator of that life, God. We have a responsibility to vote for those who will protect the unborn. I have voted pro-life in every election since I have turned eighteen and began voting. It is my responsibility.

God has spoken to me a lot about abortion throughout my life. I have never asked Him to, He just has. The most recent thing He told me was that he was bringing judgment to the people of this nation because of abortions.

He said "Summer, it is not enough that you hate abortion, and it is not enough that you vote pro-life in every election. If you want Me to protect you and your family from the things that are coming to this nation in judgment because of abortions, you must take a public stand against abortion. Then you will be sealed with protection from this judgment."

Since then, I have made sure to make a public stand against abortion. I want my family and I protected.

You may not like politics, neither do I, and you may not like public controversy I don't either, but it is our responsibility as a Christian to pray and use our vote righteously. It is another way we can be used for God.

Chapter Fourteen
For Such a Time as This

"Yet who knows whether you have come to the kingdom for such a time as this?" Esther 4:14

There are times when God uses people in extra ordinary ways. You may just be one of those people. Esther was, so was David.

Esther was in the right place at the right time to save the Jewish people from annihilation. Satan has tried throughout history to destroy the Jewish people, and this was another attempt. God saved the Jews through a woman named Esther. This is how the story goes.

Esther's Moment

King Ahasuerus, who was a powerful king, over much of the world at the time, put away his wife Queen Vashti because she disobeyed him. When his anger subsided, he missed his wife. So, his advisors came up with a plan. They told him to gather up all the beautiful young virgins in the country and put them through beauty treatments for a period of one year. Then one by one the young virgins would go into the king until he picked one that pleased him to be the new queen. {All of us ladies are groaning, but let's get on with the story.}

Esther a young Jewish girl was taken to the palace with many other young virgin girls. After her twelve months of beauty treatments, she was brought to the palace to spend the night with the king. The king was more pleased with Esther than any of the other girls. He put the royal crown on her head and proclaimed her the new queen.

Meanwhile, Haman, an evil man who was very close to the king came up with an evil plot to annihilate the Jewish people. He deceived the king, and the king signed a decree to kill the Jews on the twelfth month of that year.

Mordecai, Esther's guardian, learns of the plot and sends word of it to Esther in the palace. He wants Esther to go to the king for help. Esther tells Mordecai that she cannot go into the king unless he calls her, or she will be killed.

The king had issued a decree that anyone who enters his presence without being summoned would be killed unless he held out his scepter to them, only then would they be spared. Then she also tells Mordecai that the king had not summoned her for thirty days.

Mordecai then tells her this…. *Then Mordecai told them to answer Esther: "Do not think in your heart that you will escape in the king's palace any more than all the other Jews. For if you remain completely silent at this time, relief and deliverance will arise from the Jews from another place, but you and your father's house will perish. Yet who knows whether you have come to the kingdom for such a time as this?"*

Then Esther told them to return this answer to Mordecai: "Go gather all the Jews who are present in Shushan, and fast for me; neither eat nor drink for three days, night or day. My maids and I will fast likewise. And so, I will go to the king, which is against the law; and if I perish, I perish!" Esther 4:13-16

Esther risked her life to go before the king. Esther went into the king, and he received her, he held out his golden scepter. The story ends well Esther pleads her case before the king, the Jews are spared, and their enemy Haman is killed.

Esther was in the right place at the right time. Esther stepped out in faith, the kind of faith where she was ready to lay down her life. Esther saved the Jewish people. It was a mighty miracle. She seized her moment to do something great. She had come into the kingdom for this.

David's Moment

David is another example from the Bible of someone who was prepared and ready and in the right place at the right time.

David was a shepherd boy that spent his time tending the sheep and he had a heart for God. He was out in the fields alone but strengthening his faith. When a lion and a bear tried to kill his sheep, he bravely killed them.

During a war with the Philistines this young shepherd boy was sent by his father to bring supplies to his older brothers on the battlefield. They were soldiers. David witnessed Goliath, the giant, taunting the Israeli army as he arrived at the army camp. Goliath daily came out to challenge a man to fight him.

He said, "Choose a man for yourselves, and let him come down to me. If he is able to fight with me and kill me, then we will be your servants. But if I prevail against him and kill him, then you shall be our servants and serve us."

The Israeli army was filled with dread and fled the giant. We all know and love this story. Of course, David fights Goliath with just a sling and a stone. He kills Goliath and saves his people.

Just like Esther the situation came upon him, and he stepped out in faith ready to lay down his life and overcomes the giant. God used these two, to do extra-ordinary things, but they had to be ready to lay down their lives and step out in faith.

Who is to say that you might come into a situation where you are in the right place at the right time? You may have to risk your life, but if your heart is ready and you step out in faith, God will use you in a mighty way. You may stop an evil or save a life or many lives.

Summer's Friend

I know such a man. I am his home health aide. I learned his story one day while I was with him at his house. I was sitting on his couch looking at a scrapbook his wife had put together, and Raymond, my patient, was on the chair, near-by reading a book. Raymond was a medic in World War 2. I was reliving his life as I looked at the scrapbook. This young, nineteen-year-old boy, from Michigan, faced action over and over.

I noticed in the scrapbook a yellowed, worn, type written copy of Psalms 91 that had been with Raymond over-seas. He also carried a pocket Bible that he ended up losing on a battlefield.

Also, I noticed, that in the scrapbook were the telegrams Raymond had sent his mother home from the war. He would always say "Don't worry mom." Raymond seemed more worried about his mother than himself.

I could see this young soldier had an attitude of faith, I could tell by the letters and telegrams that he sent to his mother. Of course, Raymond carried no weapons, he was a medic; he was armed only with a type written psalm and a pocket Bible.

I turned the page of the scrapbook; on the next page was a letter of commendation by a general. Raymond had received a Silver Star medal, the highest honor for valor someone in the military can receive. I read on in amazement. Raymond, the general said, had risked his own life to save the lives of seven others. A group of soldiers were under fire and were wounded. When they tried to bring the wounded out, they discovered they were on a minefield. Each time they would try to leave to get help a mine would go off. The highest man in charge ordered the men not to move. Raymond, the nineteen-year-old medic, realized the situation and that the wounded were stranded. Risking his own life, he crossed the minefield over and over until he had brought out every wounded man.

He did what no one else there could do.

I couldn't believe it! How did he survive?

I looked up from the scrapbook over at the old man, my friend, across the room quietly reading his book. Tears were streaming from my eyes. I was sitting with a hero.

I found out more. On another occasion, Raymond was on top of a hill with other American soldiers. They were being barraged by friendly fire. Friendly fire is when you are being shot at by mistake, by your own army.

Raymond again saw the need and sprang into action again. This unarmed medic made his way down the hill as bullets whizzed past him. He barged into the commanding officers' tent and demanded "Who is in charge here?!" He told the commander they were firing on their own men. The commander immediately ordered the firing stopped.

I couldn't speak that day until just before I went home, I was too choked up. Finally, before I left, I said to Raymond, "You are awesome," then the tears started again. He just shrugged like it was nothing and smiled.

He was like David and Esther. He was a hero that was willing to lay down his life and he moved out in faith.

I have heard of other unlikely heroes in World War 2, they were two spinster women named Corrie and Betsy Ten Boom and their elderly father Casper. They lived in Holland; their father fixed clocks and had a little shop. The three of them lived together there in an apartment behind their clock shop.

When the Nazi's invaded their country, and the Jews were being taken to concentration camps, the Ten Booms became part of an underground that smuggled Jews to safety. They, like Esther, had come for such a time as this. This small Christian family acted in faith, knowing they were risking their lives.

They were caught and arrested and put in concentration camps by the Nazi's, for helping the Jewish people escape. Casper and Betsy died there. They bravely paid the ultimate price for God; they laid down their lives, in the face of evil, to save others. This is the ultimate honor for those who store their riches in Heaven.

Corrie survived. She was let out of the concentration camp because of a typographical error, just a week before all the women her age were put to death. They were a family of heroes. They didn't just stand idly by when their opportunity knocked. They were ready to step out in faith and lay their lives down for others.

You may be in a position to step out in faith; you may be put where you are for such a time as this. You may save a life or many lives, you may help someone in some way that changes their life and you may stop an evil or make a stand for righteousness.

None of these asked for these moments to come to them, but when they came, they were ready. They stood up in faith and faced their challenges. They were ready for their moment when it came. Are you ready to do something great? Could you lay down your life and step out in faith if the opportunity arose? Who knows, maybe you too have come into the kingdom for such a time as this!

Chapter Fifteen
Salt and Light

You are the salt of the earth, but if the salt loses its flavor how then shall it be seasoned? It is then good for nothing but to be thrown out and trampled underfoot by men. You are the light of the world. A city set on a hill cannot be hidden, nor do they light a lamp and put it under a basket, but on a lampstand and it gives light to all who are in the house. Let your light so shine before men that they may see your good works and glorify your Father in heaven. Matthew 5:13-16

I remember when I was a little girl seeing my mom wash and iron our dresses that my sister and I had grown out of. I'd ask her where she was taking them. {I wanted to keep them.} She would tell me she knew of someone that needed them for their little girl. That was my mom, she was always finding someone who needed something and was helping them. I don't ever remember her taking our stuff to a thrift store or trying to sell them. She would give our clothes to someone in need. That was my mom, she remembered those in need.

I remember when abortion became legal in Grand Rapids, Michigan, where we lived. My mom stood up for the unborn. She made picket signs and marched up and down in front of the abortion clinic that opened. She was joined by hundreds of others of people.

Weeks later there were only two picketers left. One was a very distinguished gentleman in a suit that walked with a cane and a briefcase. On his brief case was a bumper sticker against abortion, the other was my mom. Long after the others had given up the two of them persisted.

Then my mother put her all into backing candidates in elections that promised to get rid of abortion. She worked hard, several times I saw her on the evening news. That was my mom, she stood up for the unborn.

I also remember my mother sending a card to a man from our church that went to prison. She sent him cards regularly. He sent her a list of names of Christian inmates that needed encouragement. She found people to write to them.

Then she found out the prison didn't provide adequate winter coats for the inmates. She collected hundreds of winter coats for the men in prison, also Christian books. She got everyone at church involved. That is my mom, she remembers those in prison.

Much later when her washing machine was broken, she went across the street to a dilapidated laundry mat to wash her clothes. While she was there, she met Dorthea.

Dorthea was working at the laundry mat to support her four grandsons that she was raising alone because her daughter, their mother, had died. My mom began collecting clothes and things for these four boys she never met. Several years later I was surprised to find out she was still bringing them things; she had never stopped. That's my mom she remembers the motherless.

Through the years I remember my mom adopting older people with no family and having them for Christmas or whatever holiday. I remember her making delicious meals for single moms and their kids. Or buying an extra ham at the grocery store when they were on sale and taking them to a boy's home that was in our area. I can't even remember all the people she has helped.

And then there were the meals for the homeless. She found out a little black preacher was preaching on Sundays in the park where the homeless congregated. He would bring a pot of beans to feed the homeless people who listened to him preach. My mom found out about it and took over the food part of the service. She went to area restaurants and food places and got donations. Every Sunday she put out wonderful large meals for the homeless.

I went with her sometimes. I remember one Sunday

seeing a man lying in the grass. He was too weak to get up and get his meal. He was an alcoholic and had an empty bottle of Lysol next to him, he had drunk it. I brought him a meal my mother had prepared; he opened his eyes and weakly thanked me.

Mom fed the homeless for a long time. She even brought a homeless lady home one time and she stayed with mom for a while. That's my mom, she remembers the homeless.

Then there was Lorenzo, he was a veteran from the Korean War, he was also an alcoholic. He rode around our neighborhood on an old bike. I don't know if he had a home or not. My mother would pay him to mow her lawn. She paid him well. She didn't pay any attention to the fact that he frequently spent his wages on booze; she just treated him with the utmost respect. To her he was a war hero.

At Christmas one year, I remember her giving him a big smoked salmon and a fifty-dollar bill. Lorenzo was so happy he started dancing. He worked for mom for many years. He died young. My mom called me crying when he died, she mourned for her friend. That was my mom, she remembered the veterans.

Then there were the orphans. My daughter, Joy worked for a Christian camp for orphans one summer in the Ukraine; my brother in law had helped start it. When Joy told my mother about it, my mother became involved.

For a year my mother spent every spare minute talking to ladies' meetings and making and selling crafts, doing everything she could to raise money for the orphan camp. She paid for a large portion of the camp that year and the next and she sent every kid underwear and socks and cosmetics. Then she picked out one little orphan girl to focus on, her name was Vera. Every year my mom bought her clothes and sent her an allowance.

Vera is almost grown up now; mom still sends her money for clothes and an allowance. Vera writes to my mom to ask her help in making decisions, she calls her Grandma Peggy. She asks mom's permission on things because my mom is the person in her life that cares about her and has been there for her for years.

My mom is seventy-one years old now and she still cleans houses for a living. She is saving money for Vera because she is very worried about her leaving the orphanage and being on her own. Mom wants to save enough money to pay for her room and board with a Christian family until she can make it on her own. That is my mom, she remembers the orphans.

I wanted to tell you about my mom because she is salt, and she is light. In Satan's kingdom, the philosophy is to live for pleasure, for now, to pursue your own happiness. It is a self-centered life. My mom doesn't live this way, she lives to help others. My mom has literally touched thousands of people in her lifetime, the poor, the unborn and the elderly, those in prison, the hungry and the orphans. It is a way of life for her.

When the Son of Man comes in His glory, and all His holy angels with Him, then He will sit on the throne of His glory. All the nations will be gathered before Him, and He will separate them one from another, as a shepherd divides his sheep from the goats. And he will set the sheep on His right hand but the goats on His left. Then the King will say to those on His right hand," Come you blessed of My Father, inherit the kingdom prepared for you from the foundation of the world; for I was hungry and you gave Me food; I was thirsty and you gave Me drink: I was a stranger and you took Me in; I was naked and you clothed Me; I was sick and you visited Me; I was in prison and you came to me." Then the righteous will answer him saying, "Lord when did we see You hungry and feed You, or thirsty and give You drink? When did we see You a stranger and take You in, or naked and clothe You?" And the King will answer them and say to them "Assuredly I say to you, in as much as you did it to the least of My brethren you did it to ME" Matthew 25:31-40

Chapter Sixteen

What Am I Responsible For?

Enter by the narrow gate; for wide is the gate and broad is the way that leads to destruction, and there are many who go in by it. Because narrow is the gate and difficult is the way which leads to life, and there are few who find it Matthew 7:13-14

I was recently in a church whose pastor was doing a series of sermons on evolution. To show the effects of evolution on students, they made a video; they went into a high school and interviewed students. The video was very interesting; the subject was the meaning of life. The first question they asked the students was "Where did we come from?"

The answers varied, most tried to describe a Big Bang theory, some thought there might be a God, and some answers were so far out I don't know what they were talking about. No one's answers resembled Genesis, in the Bible. Then they asked the meaning of life. Almost every answer was the same, "To be happy" or "To find happiness." The answers varied very little. To find happiness while we are here is the supreme reason for our existence, they all thought.

The World's Mentality

This is the mentality of the world! By all means whatever it takes, find happiness.

What does that mean?

Does that mean if you fall in love with someone else's wife, you are to pursue her? After all, happiness is our number one pursuit.

Does that mean if you find yourself pregnant and a baby doesn't fit into your lifestyle, you end the child's life through abortion?

Does that mean if you are especially beautiful, and a magazine offers you a lot of money to take off all your clothes, you should go for it?

Does that mean you give yourself to whatever pleasure makes you happy, whether it is wasting your days playing video games or any other useless activity? Don't we have the right to do as we please?

Can't we spend our money as we please?

Don't I deserve to be happy?

Am I responsible to help others with my time and money? I don't want to, I work hard for my money, and I want to spend it on myself!

Why should I help feed my sister's children, when they are hungry? She married that bum of a husband; it is not my fault!

Why should I feed starving children in Africa? Those people keep having babies knowing they can't feed them.

I don't want to help my parents, or my relatives, let the government help them. Am I responsible for the poor, the sick, the weak?

I keep thinking of the rich man we read about in the book of Luke, the one who dined sumptuously, while his neighbor starved. He woke up in hell!!!

Was he responsible to help Lazarus?

Obviously, God thought he was because he woke up in

hell. There are some things we ARE responsible for, and we need to find out what they are.

The world is screaming a message at you! "Whatever makes you happy do it!"

It is the opposite message that God wants you to follow. It is a wide and easy path that leads to destruction. The rich man, in Luke, followed it and woke up in hell!

That path doesn't follow the example of Jesus Christ, who laid down His life for others, the narrow path, the difficult path, the one that leads to life.

The world's message says "It is all about here. It is all about now. Be happy and find pleasure, get money. Eat, drink and be merry for tomorrow we die."

Living Differently

We have to live differently. No, you are not responsible for everyone, but you are responsible for those God puts in your path to help. The rich man could have fed Lazarus! You can follow Christ's example. You can store up for yourself treasure in Heaven. We are not living just for here. This world is not our home.

I have a theory and it works for me. I don't think it is found in scripture, but it is good. This is it: If you can't fix your own problems, solve someone else's.

I remember when my husband and I moved into our present home, we felt we were getting in over our heads. We had been living in a nice mobile home and we loved it, but we felt the Lord told us to buy a large house. We did. It was a fixer upper.

We were worried how we were going to make the repairs. We needed a lot of money. To start with we needed a roof, a furnace and a drain-field. There was plenty more, but those things were the most important. I needed so much money it made my head swim. I shouldn't have been so worried, knowing God told us to buy this house, but I was.

I was in church on a Wednesday morning, for our prayer

meeting. It was a small group. I was feeling scared about the money I needed, it might as well have been a million dollars, it seemed like so much to me. I was kind of in shock, thinking about it. I had some money saved, a couple thousand, but nowhere near what I needed.

Sister Lucy, my little old lady friend came in. She was in the same state of mind I was. She was two hundred and fifty dollars short on her rent. It was a huge sum of money to her and may as well have been a million dollars to her, it seemed like so much. We both sat there glum.

"Wait a minute," I thought, "I can't fix my problem, but I could easily fix hers. One of us could leave here happy." So, I wrote her a check for her rent.

Do you want to know what happened to my problem? The bank appraised the house we bought for way over what we paid for it. They loaned me money to fix it up. Even though we borrowed a lot of money, our house payment went down because we got a better interest rate. I fixed sister Lucy's problem and God fixed my problem. God is good!

Sometimes you may seem so down, you don't think you can fix anyone's problem. Find a child's problem to fix, they are easier.

One time I was watching my grandson, Little David. He was so frustrated because his parent's cable had been shut off and he was trying to get the television to work. He wanted to watch his favorite cartoon. He couldn't understand why it wasn't working and he was unhappy. "I want to watch Mario," he kept saying.

Later I told my mother while we were shopping. "I have to find a Mario video for Little David. I can't fix my problem," {I can't even remember what it was now} "but I can fix his."

We went through every video in Wal-Mart, no Mario. I was determined. We stopped by my sister's house on the way home. Her son, my nephew, just happened to have a Mario video. He sold it to me for two dollars.

I fixed Little David's problem for two dollars. It may seem insignificant, but it was important to a little boy, he was happy.

Yes, we are responsible for those that God puts in our path. People don't always need money; they may be lonely or need some help you know how to do.

Yes! Yes! Yes! We are responsible for those God puts in our path. My mind just keeps going back to the rich man in Luke. Not only did he not build with things that would last, he woke up in Hell!

We need to change our philosophy; we can't listen to the message the world is screaming at us. We need to follow Christ's example. God's way is that narrow path that leads to life.

That means, take care of your responsibilities. Your first responsibilities are your own family, then, go from there.

What can I do for God? I can be responsible. I can meet the needs of those God puts in my path.

Is it not to share your bread with the hungry, And that you bring to your house the poor who are cast out; When you see the naked, that you cover him, And do not hide yourself from your own flesh? Then your light shall break forth like the morning, your healing shall spring forth speedily and your righteousness shall go before you; The glory of the Lord shall be your rear guard. Then you shall call, and the Lord will answer; you shall cry, and He will say "Here I am." Isaiah 58:7-9

Chapter Seventeen
Our Light Affliction

Therefore, we do not lose heart. Even though our outward man is perishing, yet the inward man is being renewed day by day. For our light affliction, which is but for a moment, is working for us a far more exceeding weight of glory, while we do not look at the things which are seen, but at the things which are not seen. For the things which are seen are temporary, but the things which are not seen are eternal. 2 Corinthians 4:16-18

Paul called it our light affliction. Paul the man with many afflictions. He had been put in prison. He had been shipwrecked three times. He was given the Jews thirty-nine lashes five times. He was beaten with rods three times, one time he was stoned and eventually he was martyred. And he called it our light afflictions!

Why did he call it light? Because he was comparing it to the eternal weight in glory it was working for him. There was no comparison.

Pleasing God and obedience to God isn't called difficult or the straight and narrow road for nothing. It is hard. There are afflictions. We are rowing upstream, while the world carelessly floats downstream. We choose to please God even though it means living differently. We have our eyes fixed on the unseen. It is the comparison that makes it light. The weight of glory that follows is exceeding.

A Man's Talks with Paul in Heaven

Jesse Duplantis in his book, *Heaven, Close Encounters of the God Kind,* visits heaven and he describes a conversation he had with Paul there. {Where else would Paul be?} I will quote the book.

I said to Paul, "You went through great persecution."

"Yes," he answered, "but I kept the faith. I focused my life on faith. That's how you get things done."

The next statement he made is one I have used in sermons. He said, "Our affliction is but for a moment. People have made it a lifetime. Change it back to a moment."

I get goose bumps when I think about that! It's a moment not a lifetime. "Change it back to a moment," he told me. I have used Paul's statement in seminars and people compliment me for the message, but that word didn't come from me. It came from Paul. Paul continued to speak to me, "Change it back to a moment Jesse." Then he whispered, "Change it back to a moment. Don't leave it a lifetime. I've kept the faith and that's how it's done. And it worked."

I will never forget Paul's words for as long as I live. All the troubles I have had since that trip to heaven in 1988 just roll off my back.

I have not had a life as hard as Paul's, but mine has been hard enough! Paul is telling us how he got it done. We realize they; our troubles are only for a moment! We realize they are light compared to the eternal weight of glory. We need to focus on all God has done for us and realize He is not finished; He will continue to work. What we focus on becomes bigger. Do we focus on what God has already done for us or do we focus on our problems?

A Lesson from an Angel

This reminds me of something else I read in a book. {Yes, another book, sorry, I am a book worm.}

This was Pastor Roland Buck's book again, *Angels on Assignment,* which I quoted earlier in this book. As you already know Pastor Buck was visited by angels and taught many wonderful truths. In this portion of the book, which I will quote here, the angel Gabriel draws him a little picture and gives him a little lesson.

Another of the many beautiful truths through the mouth of the angel Gabriel was that everything God has promised is already completed as far as God's book in Heaven is concerned. This statement was very difficult for me to understand, so Gabriel took a pencil which I held in my hand and drew a rough sketch of a picture frame. Everything God has promised is complete in this picture. But he said, "Here is a tiny little spot representing things that are unclear to you-things not yet complete. You often spend your time looking at these things until the tiny spot expands outward and fills the frame, and totally hides what God has done. If you look to Jesus instead of the problem, you will see the complete picture."

In Isaiah 43:2 The Lord said, "When you go through deep waters and great trouble, I will be with you." If you look at the waters of trouble, it will hide the picture, but if you look to Jesus, that little piece that looks so ominous has to shrink back to place and then you will see the whole picture complete with everything that God has promised.

We are not to focus on our trials. We are to focus on God, what he has done and what he has promised to do. We are to realize that our trials are light and that we have an eternal weight of glory coming.

Count it all Joy

I have had much trouble in my life. I hate trouble! I hate trouble! I hate trouble! I want to be done with it forever! {That day will come.} I have been going through a lot of trouble lately and right in the thick of it I read this.

My brethren count it all joy when you fall into various trials, knowing that the testing of your faith produces patience. But let patience have its perfect work, that you may be perfect and complete lacking nothing. James 1:2-4

I read that verse, a verse I have read countless times, and all of a sudden it dawned on me, the Bible is serious. I am really supposed to count it all joy when I am going through this awful stuff. I am actually supposed to do this; I am supposed to rejoice when I fall into various trials.

I tried it. This is new; this is different, looking at trials in a different light. It takes some practice. This patience stuff, that we have to go through trials to get, it is supposed to make us perfect and complete, lacking nothing.

I am recommending that you try this. It is part of focusing on the unseen. Realizing that we are to think differently about trials and that we are to count it all joy. First, we are to consider our trials light and only for a moment and now we are actually rejoicing in them.

Guess what? It feels better to be in faith than in fear. It feels better to rejoice than to cry. {I get a headache when I cry.} Trials look tiny when you focus on eternity and all God has done for you already. Paul lived through greater afflictions than many of us will have to and he called them light. He made them a moment. We can do this too! Does this please God? Yes!

Chapter Eighteen
God Never Wastes Anything

And we know that all things work together for good to those who love God, to those who are the called according to His purpose Romans 8:28

This chapter is about suffering. It is never wasted. I think that I have cried more tears in my life than the average person.

I have been married to my husband Jim for thirty-three years. My husband came through much abuse and became addicted to alcohol and drugs at an early age. Our life together has been very difficult. I knew God put us together, but it was a narrow road filled with much suffering. Tears were part of my daily existence. As the years kept passing, I wondered if my life was just going to be about suffering. I sometimes felt like my life was wasted.

Then I would tell myself, "I have given my life to God, and I have followed Him and if He wants to waste my life it is

His to waste." I wondered if the Lord would ever use me.

Summer's Desert

For many years, in prayer, I saw myself in a desert. I had been crossing this desert for years. This desert was very real to me. I prayed and cried my way across the desert; I knew the end would have to come someday. One, two, three, five, ten, twenty years and more went by and I was still crying my way across this desert. I would weep and pray and weep and pray as I crossed this wilderness.

One day I was in my desert, crying and praying again, and looking ahead wondering where the end would be, then after all those years I turned around and looked back behind me. I had never done that before.

I gasped in amazement.

There was no desert behind me. Behind me was a beautiful garden; as far as I could see was lush beautiful scenery.

"Lord," I asked amazed, "Where is the desert?"

"Summer," the Lord answered me gently, "It is a garden now. You have watered it with your tears."

Of course, this is a place in my heart that belongs to the Lord. But I was learning something; the Lord doesn't waste anything, not our suffering, not a single tear drop, not anything we go through. We are so precious to Him; He will not waste anything. So many times, through the years the devil has been right there telling me to quit; nothing was ever going to change. I didn't quit.

Suffering Brings Authority

Suffering is not looked on by God the same way we see it. Suffering causes promotion in the Kingdom of Heaven. In my favorite book, the *Final Quest,* written by Rick Joyner, he talks about suffering. The book is a prophetic vision and in the book the author, Rick, is in a spiritual battle and he is having a conversation with an eagle which I believe represents those with a prophetic gifting. Rick was thinking about the people who had been wounded in the battle on the level of the mountain called salvation. The eagle as if reading his thoughts begins to explain to him about suffering. I will quote this wonderful passage on suffering.

"God has a different definition of peace and safety than we do. To be wounded in the fight is a great honor. It is by the Lord's stripes that we are healed, and it is through our stripes that we, too, are given the authority for healing. In the very place that the enemy wounds us, once we are healed, we are given the power to heal others. Healing was a basic part of the Lord's ministry, and it is also a basic part of ours. That is one reason why the Lord allows bad things to happen to His people, so that they can receive the compassion for others by which the power of healing operates. That is why the apostle Paul told of his beatings and stoning when his authority was questioned. Every wound, every bad thing that happens to us, can be turned into the authority to do good. Every beating that the great apostle took resulted in salvation for others. Every wound that every warrior takes will result in others being saved, healed, or restored." "Until you have beheld and appreciated the depths of the treasures of salvation, you cannot see the glory that comes from suffering for the sake of the gospel. Once you have seen it, you are ready for the tests that will release you for the highest levels of spiritual authority in your life. These scars are the glory that we will carry forever. This is why even the wounds our Lord suffered are with Him in heaven. You can still see His wounds, and the wounds that all of his chosen have taken for His sake. These are the medals of Honor in heaven.

I love this wonderful passage from this wonderful book. It was changing the way I looked at suffering; it was changing how I looked at my life. In the very areas we suffer, we receive authority to help others once we are healed, how exciting. There is glory from suffering. Our suffering is not wasted, just as Jesus stripes were not wasted, they bought our healing.

God had not wasted my life; my suffering was not in vain.

The Ark of the Covenant

God added more to what He was teaching me on suffering and that He doesn't waste anything in a sermon at church one Sunday night. Our pastor loves archeology and studies it as it pertains to the Bible.

This particular Sunday night our pastor spoke about the Ark of the Covenant. Remember that from the Old Testament, the Ark of the Covenant was in the Holy of holies in the temple. Only the high priest could go in there once a year, and he would put blood on the mercy seat of the Ark of the Covenant. He would put the blood of a spotless lamb.

There are many amazing stories about the Ark of the Covenant in the Bible.

The Ark of the Covenant disappeared around 586 B.C. when the temple was destroyed. During Jesus time, the Ark of the Covenant was still missing, this was something that seemed wasted to me and unfinished. But it wasn't wasted God knew exactly where that Ark of the Covenant was, and He fulfilled its purpose.

Our pastor was telling us, in his sermon, about a man named Ron Wyatt. He was a nurse, but in his spare time was an archaeologist in the holy land. He has had many amazing finds. During the period of 1979-1981 Ron was in Jerusalem looking for the Ark of the Covenant. The whole story is written on his website, but I am going to condense it here.

Ron began his excavation at the base of the skull face at Golgotha, where Jesus was crucified. As he excavated down, he found a niche in the rock he believed this to be the actual crucifixion site.

He found three smooth places on the rock wall behind the niches where he believed the signs were hung behind the crosses in three languages.

Pilate had hung a sign behind Jesus' cross that read, "The King of the Jews." There was also evidence that an early church met at this site.

In the ground at this level, were square holes in the ground about twenty-three- and one-half inches deep that he believed was where they put the crosses in the ground. One of the cross holes, the center one, had a deep crevice that appeared to have been made by an earthquake.

Later they found a cave directly under this crack and the square hole, which was for the crosses. There was a network of caves and tunnels under ground that were from the original temple, from Solomon's time.

Ron was able to make a small opening into one of these caves. He was working from the crucifixion site. Ron could just barely squeeze into the opening. The cave had been packed with rocks and things wrapped in old animal skins that crumbled when he moved them. Under the crumbling animal skins, he found gold items from the temple, the lampstand, the table, these things.

He looked up and saw the crack in the earth that came from the center cross hole, the crevice from an earthquake caused a crack from the cross hole down through the earth and into the cave.

He believed this particular hole to be the cross hole that was Christ's.

As Ron saw the crack, he also saw a black substance coming down from the crack and into the cave. He crawled over to where the black substance had flowed down through the crack and there, he found the Ark of the Covenant!

Ron realized this black substance was literally the blood of Jesus! As Jesus hung on the cross dying, there was an earthquake that literally opened up the earth and allowed His blood to flow from the cross onto the mercy seat of the Ark of the Covenant, fulfilling the sacrifice for all time!

Jesus was the true spotless Lamb of God. The ark had been hidden carefully in a cave, centuries before, by one of the prophets, to keep it safe from the Babylonians. Only God knew it was directly under the cross of Christ.

God does not waste anything! He carefully orchestrates everything whether we know it or not, He fulfills His purposes. Ron Wyatt actually scraped up some of the blood he found and had it tested. When he did, they made some remarkable discoveries; it only had half of the chromosomes and it was still alive!!!!

I think it is also an amazing fact that the blood of Christ began at the skull, Golgotha, a hill called the skull, but fell to the heart of the earth. {We need to come to the Lord with more than our heads, He needs to penetrate to our hearts.}

When Ron realized he was actually seeing the blood of Christ and the Ark of the Covenant, he was overcome! He passed out in the cave for about forty-five minutes!

When I heard our pastor tell this awesome story I didn't pass out, but the tears began to flow for the rest of the day, and my heart burned. I spent the remainder of the day in a daze, a daze of wonder at the goodness of God. I was so in awe of how God fulfilled the sacrifice of the blood of Jesus onto the mercy seat of the Ark of the Covenant that it took my breath away, and I was moved to tears.

The Israeli government immediately shut down Ron Wyatt's excavation when they heard what he had found. I believe in God's appointed time the Ark of the Covenant will be brought out. Ron Wyatt has since passed away.

God doesn't waste anything, not your suffering and not one drop of Jesus' blood. Remember God doesn't see suffering the way we do.

If your life is in God's hands and you are following Him, nothing you are going through will be wasted.

Your suffering brings promotion in the kingdom of God.

Your suffering gives you authority to minister to others.

Jesus' suffering resulted in our salvation!

God will not waste your suffering and He WILL fulfill His purposes for you.

Chapter Nineteen
So, Can God Use Me?

One of His disciples, Andrew, Simon Peter's brother, said to Him, "There is a lad here who has five barley loaves and two small fish, but what are they among so many?
And Jesus said, "Make the people sit down." Now there was much grass in the place. So, the men sat in number about five thousand. And Jesus took the loaves, and when He had given thanks, He distributed them to the disciples and the disciples to those sitting down; and likewise of the fish, as much as they wanted. And when they were filled, He said to the disciples, "Gather up the fragments that remain, so that nothing is lost." Therefore, they gathered them up and filled twelve baskets with the barley loaves which were left over by those who had eaten. John 6:8-13

I really wanted to be used by God. I was waiting for Him to make me into a Billy Graham, a super soul winner who changes the world. But that was the imaginary Summer. The one who read all the Christian biographies and thought her life was going to be grand. I thought that God was going to do this big thing in me and make me great for Him. The imaginary me could stand before millions and preach marvelous sermons. The real me was shy.

I have always been shy. I hate attention. I don't know why. I remember in third grade when one of the little girls in my class, for her birthday, took all her friends to the Buck Berry Show. It was a local show in our area, Grand Rapids, Michigan, which we all watched after school. It had a studio audience of kids. As I was sitting on the bleachers in that studio audience, I saw that television camera coming my way I wanted to hide. Every time it came my way I looked up or down or to the side. I couldn't stand to be seen.

On the way home, the mother who brought us all had noticed, she said, "Every time the camera came to Summer, she was looking the other way."

I cringed. The imaginary me was a movie star, the real me couldn't stand to be seen.

So, I was waiting for God to make me into something else. I thought God was going to take me high; do something great with my life. I came to God at fourteen. He had my whole life ahead to use me and do something great!

Instead, He took me low.

He took me by the way of suffering, and service.

Life was too much for me. I became a wife and a mother, but it was still too much. I was so dysfunctional and so was my husband. I tell our story in my book, *The Impossible Marriage.* Our marriage was impossible because we were two broken people.

My husband Jim was an ex-convict and an alcoholic who had a lifetime of abuse behind him. I was equally dysfunctional; I was so shattered inside that my personality was nonexistent. For many years my life seemed unbearable.

But I still kept thinking a God was going to do a miracle and change us in an instant. We would go to the altar and get prayer and God was going instantly fix us. There was still time. But the years passed, and I lived in my desert, my desert of tears. I kept moving forward but there was no end in sight. I didn't know a garden was growing behind me.

For years I thought that somehow God's will for my life

had somehow been aborted. That God had a wonderful plan but somehow, He just wasn't able to pull it off. Somehow, we just missed it. I thought my life was going to be one way and instead it was totally the opposite.

I have since learned better. I realized God had some more important things on His agenda, more important than making my life glorious. I thought my life had been wasted but it hadn't been. Remember God doesn't waste anything. My life was about something else. It was about the image of Christ being formed in me, in my husband, and in our children.

I thought I had to achieve a life of works for God. I wanted to be a super saint. But God has been doing a work in me. I didn't see it.

I have also learned something else, about what I can do for God. It is not so much what I can do. It is what He can do through me. You see, it will always be His plan, His work, and His way. All my plans seem to come to nothing.

Remember Moses? His plans came to nothing, at first. He wanted to help his people who were slaves in Egypt and ended up killing someone. He saw an Egyptian beating a Hebrew slave and he killed him. He ended up fleeing for his life and spending forty years in the desert in Midian before God called Him from the burning bush. Moses saw his life come to nothing. But that is it, it is God's work not our own. It was God's plan Moses followed, not his own.

Jesus' life was viewed by many of His time to be wasted. He walked a narrow path through life that led to suffering and a cross and death. But that was God's plan! God's perfect plan!

God sees things differently than I do! His plans look different than mine! Seemingly wasted lives are not wasted! God hadn't aborted His plan for my life, or Moses life either and especially not Jesus' life.

It is God's plan for my life and the outcome is in His hands. My job is to follow Him.

Remember the story of Jesus feeding the five thousand? What did He use, a chef, or a world-famous cook?

No, the disciples found a little boy who had a lunch packed, a couple of fish and some bread. The little boy gave his lunch. God took a little boy's lunch and multiplied it.

He uses humble things.

I have given my life to God. God will take this seemingly wasted life of mine and use it, His way. My life is like the little boy's lunch. It is God's to do with as He pleases.

Remember my seemingly futile effort to talk to Sam, my mother's next-door neighbor that I wrote about in the beginning of this book? I was so devastated at my attempt to reach him I didn't want to come out of my house for days. Eventually I put it behind me and moved on, although I never tried to speak to him again. I forgot about it, but Sam didn't.

Apparently, God pricked his heart. A neighbor told me months later Sam felt terrible for the way he treated me. Apparently, it was still on his mind because he told her about it. Maybe the couple of words I managed to get out affected him. I can't tell you the end of the story because I don't know, we moved away. But maybe God used me after all.

Chapter Twenty
The Bigger Picture

For a day in Your courts is better than a thousand. I would rather be a doorkeeper in the house of my God than dwell in the tents of wickedness. Psalms 84:10

Dear Friends,

In this book, I have tried to answer the question, What can I do for God? When I first became a Christian, I had a picture what a Christian should be, something like Billy Graham.

I am nothing like Billy Graham. I have since learned that God has made me unique. He has made each of us unique. He has a plan for our lives that we fit into perfectly. There is more to pleasing God than I thought, and it is possible for me and you too.

Some of the things I have covered are:

I have learned that to love God is our first priority, not only to love Him but to become Christ like. To become like Christ was more important for me than to become the superstar Christian I thought I had to become.

I have learned He will use my life for His will, His way.

I have learned that my attitude is important and how much effort I put forth.

I have learned that being a good mate is my service to

Him and being a good parent is my service to Him, that I need to honor my parents and be concerned for my family.

I have learned that God has put people on my path that I am responsible for.

I have learned to look at things differently than the world has taught me to. I have learned that my real security is in God and not money, or houses or stuff. Worldly security is like building castles in the sand. I am not here for pleasure or to save for retirement or even to take the easy road through life.

I am here to follow Jesus down a narrow road, to a cross and to eternal life. I don't need to be beautiful or young, I don't need plastic surgery or go to the gym every day, it is not required, and God values my heart.

I see that suffering has a reason and I don't need to be afraid of it.

I need to see the bigger picture. I need to see things from God's perspective. I need to realize the bigger picture is eternity, forever. I will be there soon and so will you. There are things that carry eternal importance, things that last; these are the treasures we can store in Heaven. It takes looking up; it takes keeping focused on the bigger picture. Heaven is the bigger picture. Heaven is the real world, the one that lasts forever. Both Heaven and Hell are eternal, forever.

We put so much importance on the job we are going to do for thirty or forty years, the job we do in this life. We study for it; plan for it, our career here, is the focus of many people's lives. What job are we going to do until we retire? Others of us hate our jobs but we endure them.

Have you ever wondered what you will be doing forever? Have you ever thought that the things you are going through are preparing you for the occupation you will be doing forever? Those who prove themselves will hold positions of great responsibility and honor on an eternal basis.

We also focus on the place we live for this short time on earth, we want dream houses, matching furniture, good neighborhoods, and perfect yards. But what about where you will be living forever? Shouldn't that be of more importance?

Have you ever thought that some of the things you are going through in this life may be preparing you for the bigger picture, your eternal position? We are going to be living in a world that works together in perfect unity and you have a role in that world. God not only has a plan for this short little vapor we call life on earth; He has a forever plan for you. You were created for a purpose in an eternal scheme.

I have always wondered if I will be dancing in Heaven. I have always loved to dance. If I hear music, it is hard for me to hold still. I love to dance while I worship God. I believe this is something God made me for and although I am no ballerina on earth, I will be dancing in Heaven because it is part of who God made me. I am going to love dancing before His throne.

Life has a bigger picture, and the bigger picture is Heaven. This is why our life on earth is so much more important than we can possibly realize. What we do has eternal consequences, for us, for our mates, for our children and grandchildren and for those God has called us to help. I want to be faithful in all God has for me to do.

We try to figure things out, but we only look at the smaller picture. We always think of death as a tragedy, but have you ever considered that God may take someone off this earth to fill a need in the real world, the one that lasts forever?

No one likes to go through trials, but have you ever thought the trials you go through are building in you a strong character, so you can be usable by God in an eternal plan?

So many of us on earth focus our lives on money and getting rich, but money is not part of the bigger picture. God doesn't call the things on earth, like money and silver and gold true riches. The wealth that is in Heaven is what true riches are.

What we call riches on earth is like children playing with Monopoly money. It is not real. Oh, it helps you win a short {or not so short} little game. You can buy little green houses and little red hotels, but it's all a game, not real, it's over soon. Then it is worthless, when the game is over.

Do you realize that the time we spend on earth compared to the time we spend in eternity is just a tiny speck of time, like the time we spend playing Monopoly compared to the rest of our life? Monopoly money doesn't compare to our currency, neither does our currency compare to true heavenly riches.

It is not worth spending the focus of your life upon, it is not worth fighting over or cheating or stealing to get it and it is certainly not worth your soul.

We have a life ahead of us that never ends. Heaven is a real world. We all know people who are there right now, grandmas and grandpas, aunts and uncles. Their lives have continued there.

There are homes in heaven, schools in heaven, occupations and duties to perform in heaven. The difference is they are absolutely joyful and fulfilling. Heaven has places to visit and goods to exchange, places of beauty to visit. There are even theme parks. It is a wonderful place!

But it gets better yet, because we will see God in heaven, and we will see Jesus and be able to talk with Him face to face. We will no longer walk by faith but by sight. The absolute epitome of the universe, and the epitome of our lives, our eternal lives, will be experienced in heaven. And that is to come to the Throne of God. To stand before the Throne of God, worshipping there and having a place to call your own in that massive place where the universe is run.

This is the place where every created being originated from the Father, from His thoughts, in that eternal, holy place, it is the highest place, the most holy place and the most wonderful place to be. No wonder King David said it is better to spend one day in the house of the Lord than a thousand elsewhere and that he would rather be a doorkeeper in the house of the Lord than to dwell in the tents of the wicked. The very lowest place in heaven is better than the very highest place on earth.

God is beginning to reveal eternity to us. The veil between Heaven and earth is getting thinner.

It is ridiculous to think we do not know what happens to us after we die. First of all, the Bible has much to say about heaven and hell. Also, God has brought many people there in every generation to witness heaven and hell and come back to tell us of the wonders of heaven and warn us of the horrors of hell. There are many books out there about it and I have tried to read every one of them.

What could be more important than learning about eternity? There are many fakes, but they are easy to spot because we are told so much about heaven and hell in the Bible.

I love testimonies of heaven; they get me looking up. I don't especially like testimonies of hell, but they give me perspective and keep me repentant.

I remember about fourteen or fifteen years ago my sister called me and told me there is a video out about a man who visited Heaven, she had seen it, she told me his name was Jessie Duplantis. I immediately ordered the video. It was called *Close Encounters of the God Kind*. I have always been on a tight budget but things like that go to the top of my priority list.

We got the video, and my family watched it over and over. My middle girl, Lonna was maybe thirteen; she would watch it every day after school, over and over. She told me, "I can go through anything at school during the day because I know when I get home, I know I am going to watch the video about heaven." It got her looking up; it got her looking at the bigger picture.

It is okay to think about our home, heaven. It is okay to live your life, looking toward the goal, the finish line. It is okay to live for the day you stand before the Throne of God and face your Creator. That day will come. It is okay to base your life on hearing the words He will speak to you if you live your life for Him.

"Well done my good and faithful servant."

I want you to know what you can do for God, what pleases Him and how you can do the things that last. I want to leave you looking at the bigger picture. I want to leave you looking up.

Love your sister in Christ, Summer

Epilogue

"Behold, I stand at the door and knock. If anyone hears My voice and opens the door, I will come into him and dine with him and he with Me."
Jesus
{Revelation 3:20}

If you somehow made it through this book and you don't know Jesus, this epilogue is for you. The most important event in history is Jesus dying on the cross for our sins. The most important decision and event in our lives is whether we receive that salvation or not. It determines our destiny for eternity. You can do this right now.

The moment I gave my heart to Jesus, when I was fourteen years old, changed everything for me. I went from darkness to light in a moment's time. I didn't pray a prayer I just hollered out "I want God!" He heard me and Jesus changed me in that instant. The words you say are not the most important thing; the important thing is your heart.

Do you want to receive the price Jesus paid for you? Do you want the author of peace, joy and love to live in your heart? Do you want to be right with God and call Him Father? Do you want to become a citizen of heaven? You can through Jesus.

Pray this prayer

Dear Jesus, I need You; I want You. Please forgive my sins and come into my heart. Be my Lord and Savior, I give myself to You.   Amen.

Therefore, if anyone is in Christ, he is a new creation; old things have passed away; behold all things have become new. 2 Corinthians 5:17

Notes

Chapter 2 .... *The Call* by Rick Joyner, copyright 1999

www.morningstarministries.org
pages 201-202

Chapter 3....Bob Jones, Vision of Heaven and Hell

The Cross and the Switchblade, by David Wilkerson

Chapter4....*Paradise the Holy City and the Glory of the Throne* by Rev. Elwood Scott Engeltal Press Jasper, Arkansas   page 10

Angels on Assignment by Charles and Frances Hunter as told by Roland Buck Hunter Books Kingwood, Texas
page 137

Chapter 5.... *The Heavens Opened* by Anna Rountree Creation House Lake Mary, Florida   pages 11-12

Chapter 7....*A Very Present Help*
Guideposts Carmel New York
The Bachelor Husband by Calvin Kinzie page 181

Chapter 14...*The Hiding Place* by Corrie Ten Boom

Chapter 17...*Heaven Close Encounters of the God Kind* by Jesse Duplantis Harrison House Tulsa, Oklahoma pages 97-98

Angels on Assignment by Charles and Frances Hunter as told by Roland Buck Hunter Books Kingwood, Texas page 43

Chapter 18....*The Final Quest* by Rick Joyner
copyright 1996 used by permission
,www.morningstarministries.org
Pages 78-80

Ron Wyatt

www.wyattmuseum.com/arkofthecovenant.htm

All scripture references are New King James version

Thomas Nelson Inc. 1982

www.ingramcontent.com/pod-product-compliance
Lightning Source LLC
Chambersburg PA
CBHW051812040426
42446CB00007B/630